MW01198977

GREAT
~~INDIAN~~
CHILDREN'S
STORIES

GREAT INDIAN CHILDREN'S STORIES

Edited by
Stephen Alter

a

ALEPH

ALEPH

ALEPH BOOK COMPANY
An independent publishing firm
promoted by *Rupa Publications India*

First published in India in 2022
by Aleph Book Company
7/16 Ansari Road, Daryaganj
New Delhi 110 002

ISBN: 978-93-91047-63-4

1 3 5 7 9 10 8 6 4 2

Printed at Parksons Graphics Pvt. Ltd, Mumbai

CONTENTS

STORIES OF CHILDHOOD

STEPHEN ALTER

Everyone grows up with stories, whether these are told by parents and grandparents, or heard from other narrators, including a range of garrulous electronic devices available today. Some of our earliest memories revolve around stories that we absorbed while learning our first language, words fitting together in patterns that allowed us to comprehend the world into which we were born. Many of these early recollections become the germs of tales that we tell ourselves and others, again and again, as we grow older, interpreting and reinterpreting their meaning at different stages of our lives. In this way, each of us assembles his or her own personal anthology of anecdotes, riddles, fables, dreams, and myths. Ultimately, we are the product of the multitude of stories embedded in our individual and collective imaginations.

India possesses a vast and varied landscape of stories dating back over several millennia. During the eleventh century, an attempt was made to compile these into a single anthology, called the *Kathasaritsagara*, or 'Ocean of Stories'. Of course, even an encyclopaedic compendium like this represents only a small part of our storytelling heritage. Much older than the *Kathasaritsagara* are the Mahabharata and Ramayana epics, which are complex story cycles that were woven together from a time before recorded history began. In addition to these are compilations of Buddhist fables and allegories like the *Panchatantara*, which continue to fascinate and instruct us on a spiritual as well as a practical plane. Various streams of storytelling converge in India's oceanic narratives, from Sufi parables like 'The Conference of Birds', to the myths and folklore of numerous languages like Tamil, Kannada, or Bengali. Every region, from the Himalaya to the Nilgiris, from the Malabar coast to the Bay of Bengal, has its own storehouse of legends and folk tales, some of which are unique and others very similar. Today, with the fluidity of the internet and social media, more and more of these stories are being shared across cultural and geographical boundaries, so that tales from Assam or Nagaland are retold in Maharashtra or Gujarat.

When we speak of 'Children's Stories' there is something inherently ambiguous and even paradoxical about such a literary genre or classification. Some may argue that children's stories must be exclusively for younger readers and listeners, which carries with it judgemental dictates about acceptable subjects, themes, and language. However, the truth is that almost any good story that will appeal to a younger audience probably contains elements that protective adults are likely to consider inappropriate. That's because a successful story disturbs or startles us out of the safe and complacent cocoons of our minds. Whether it is ghosts, witches, or other hints of violence and evil, the things we try to shield children from are often exactly what they want or need to know.

Some of the most enduring fairy tales are full of dangerous and fearsome creatures, as well as situations that arouse anxiety. In some cases, these are cautionary tales, with the purpose of teaching children to beware of predatory individuals or self-destructive behaviour. The moral of the story is delivered as a finger-wagging lesson, warning us that bad things befall those who fail to heed instructions given by adults. For obvious reasons, I've always found those kinds of stories boring. Even at an early age, I was captivated by characters, situations, and events that didn't fit neatly into a convenient box and weren't tied up with a sanctimonious ribbon. Instead, it was much more interesting to hear or read a story that ended with a question, or that left things unresolved.

For instance, the ancient fable of 'Little Red Riding Hood', which comes to us in various versions, including a German retelling by the Brothers Grimm, is a story full of uncertainty and violence. A young girl is sent off alone into the forest, by her mother, to deliver food to her grandmother. She is pursued by a hungry wolf, who first gobbles Granny up and then puts on the old woman's clothes, after which he deceives the girl and eats her up too. In most versions, a hunter or a woodsman arrives before the girl and her grandmother have been fully digested and the wolf is cut open, to save his two hapless victims. Naturally, this fable left me with a lot of questions, many of which I still haven't completely unravelled. Another folk tale that I heard as a child growing up in India was the story of the churail, a mysterious woman— sometimes young and beautiful, sometimes an old hag. She was capable of powerful magic and preyed upon innocent young children, emitting bloodcurdling screams. Her feet were twisted around at the ankles, pointing backwards, so that if anyone tried to chase after her, attempting to rescue her victims, they would follow her footprints in the wrong direction. Sixty years after I first heard of churails, I still puzzle over the anatomy of evil and where it actually leads us.

Modern stories that are written and published, as against those that come from an oral tradition, represent a more formal and rigid approach to narration. In most cases, the words on the page have not been passed down from one storyteller to the next, with added embellishments and digressions. Instead, they are conceived as original tales that are carefully crafted and edited, to give them literary qualities. Storybooks for younger children are often intended to be read aloud by a parent or an older sibling. Yet, once the child begins to read for herself or himself, it becomes a solitary, sometimes secret pursuit. Imagined landscapes are revealed, peopled with exotic characters and full of exciting, confusing encounters. Young readers are often more attentive and critical than adults because they invest a greater part of their imaginations in the stories they choose. They are also more willing to explore subjects and plot lines that mature readers find either fanciful or absurd. As a rule, the older we get the less willing we are to accept stories that are 'make believe', though we have concocted a more intellectual term, 'the suspension of disbelief', to allow us access to fictional worlds. At the end of the day, it's all the same thing, using words and images to kindle and ignite our imaginations in order to escape the mundane routines of our everyday lives and enter a more inviting, alternate reality.

⌁

The stories in this collection are almost all from the twentieth century. Some of them, like Rabindranath Tagore's 'The Kabuliwallah' and Premchand's 'Idgah' are considered classics. Several, like Ruskin Bond's 'The Blue Umbrella', have been adapted as films. In one way or another, each of these stories revolves around the idea of growing up and many contain a moment of epiphany when the child sees the world, for the first time, through the eyes of an adult. It is often a poignant moment, sometimes alarming, and generally tinged with sadness or nostalgia.

Growing up, or 'coming of age' as it is sometimes called, is fundamentally a tragic experience. We leave behind the joys and pleasures of childhood and face the future with the knowledge that nothing will ever be quite the same. Nevertheless, as we progress through successive strata of maturity, we carry our stories with us to remind us of the awe and wonder we experienced while listening to or reading these colourful mosaics of words that touched us with fear and laughter, astonishment, and desire.

This collection is intended for mature children and young adults, as well as older readers too. If the subjects or themes worry parents or teachers, in one way or another, it is probably because the writer has succeeded in touching a nerve that takes them back to their own childhood. That germ of a story that you recognize as your own cannot be sanitized or disinfected. No vaccine or antibiotic exists that can protect or sterilize our imaginations. Psychologists tell us that our earliest memories influence our behaviour and personalities. It could be argued that everything we recollect becomes part of the conscious or subconscious anthologies that we arrange and edit in our minds.

Instead of an 'Ocean of Stories', I prefer to think of India's vast and seemingly limitless repertoire of tales as being more like the monsoon. These days we speak of saving information in 'the cloud', though my simile doesn't come from digital storage, but instead from the ancient Sanskrit bard and playwright, Kalidasa. His famous narrative poem, *Meghaduta*, 'The Cloud Messenger', is based on a multilayered and lyrical metaphor in which the poet imagines a narrator—dark as a monsoon cloud and shaped like an elephant— drifting across the sky and releasing its stories upon the land. Sometimes they fall as gentle showers bringing fertility to the soil while at other times they pour down like a deluge, flooding the earth.

The modern tales of childhood in this book represent only a miniscule and selective fraction of Indian storytelling, like a few raindrops amidst a prolonged downpour. Yet, in subtle, invisible ways, each story carries with it and precipitates a condensed memory of those monsoon clouds. Borne by restless breezes across a diverse subcontinent of people and places, these stories remind us of who we are and where we grew up.

THE KABULIWALLAH

RABINDRANATH TAGORE

Translated from the Bengali by Arunava Sinha

My five-year-old daughter talked all the time. It had taken her a year after her birth to master the language, and since then she has not wasted a second of her waking hours in silence. Although her mother often hushed her, this was beyond me. A silent Mini was so unnatural a being that I could not bear it for long. So, I always encouraged her to prattle on.

I had barely started the seventeenth chapter of my novel that morning when Mini appeared by my side and began chattering at once, 'Ramdayal, the doorman, calls the crow kauwa instead of kaak, Baba, he just doesn't know anything, does he?'

Before I could talk about linguistic diversity, she had moved to another subject. 'Baba, Bhola says it rains because elephants spray water with their trunks from the sky. He talks such rubbish, my god. He keeps talking, talks all the time.'

Without pausing for my opinion, Mini suddenly asked, 'What relation is Ma to you, Baba?'

'Shaali,' I answered to myself. To Mini I said, 'Go play with Bhola, Mini. I'm busy.'

Flopping down by my feet next to the desk, she began to play a game involving her knees and hands, accompanied by a rhyme uttered at express velocity. In the seventeenth chapter of my novel, Pratap Singh was about to leap with Kanchanmala in his arms from the high window of the prison into the river flowing below.

My room looked out on the street. Mini abruptly stopped her game to rush to the window and began to shout, 'Kabuliwallah, Kabuliwallah.'

A tall Kabuliwallah—one of those hawkers of dry fruits who came all the way from Afghanistan to make a living in Calcutta—was walking slowly up the road, a turban on his head, a bag slung over his shoulder, holding two or three boxes of grapes. It was difficult to say what emotions he aroused in my daughter, but she continued to call out to him breathlessly. I was afraid that if the wily peddler with a bag of things to sell came into my room, I could bid goodbye to any prospect of finishing chapter seventeen that day.

The Kabuliwallah turned and smiled at Mini's shouts and began walking towards our house. Her courage gave way and she ran from the room at great speed, vanishing into the house. She was convinced that if the

Kabuliwallah's bag was opened and examined, it would reveal three or four children just like her.

Meanwhile, the man himself appeared, offering me a smiling salute. Although Pratap Singh and Kanchanmala were in dire straits, I reflected that it would be discourteous to invite him into the house and buy nothing.

I bought a few things and we began chatting. We exchanged notes on frontier policies involving Abdur Rahman, the Russians, and the English.

When he was about to leave, the Kabuliwallah finally asked, 'Where did your daughter go, Babu?'

I sent for Mini in order to dispel her fears. Pressing herself to me, Mini cast suspicious glances at the Kabuliwallah and his large bag. He offered her some raisins and dry fruit, but she simply wouldn't accept them, holding my knee tightly. And there the first meeting between them ended.

A few days later, when I was about to leave the house on an errand, I discovered my daughter seated on the bench next to the front door, chattering away to the Kabuliwallah who sat at her feet, listening smilingly, and occasionally saying something in broken Bengali. Mini had never encountered such an attentive listener in the five years of her life besides her father. I even found nuts and raisins bundled into the aanchal of her tiny sari. 'Why have you given her all this?' I asked the Kabuliwallah. 'Don't do it again.' Taking an eight-anna coin out of my pocket, I handed it to him. He accepted it without demur, putting it in his bag.

I returned home to find the eight-anna coin at the heart of a hundred rupees worth of trouble.

Holding a circular, silvery object in her hand, Mini's mother was asking her daughter disapprovingly, 'Where did you get this?'

'The Kabuliwallah gave it to me,' Mini told her.

'Why did you have to take it from him?' Mini's mother inquired.

'I didn't want to, he gave it on his own,' Mini said, on the verge of tears.

I rescued Mini from imminent danger and took her outside.

There I learnt that it wasn't as though this was only Mini's second meeting with Rahmat, the Kabuliwallah. He had been coming to see her almost every day, bribing her with almonds and raisins to conquer her tiny, greedy five-year-old heart.

I observed that the two friends had established an easy familiarity between themselves, sharing private jokes and quips. For instance, on spotting Rahmat, my daughter would ask, laughing, 'What's in that bag of yours, Kabuliwallah?'

In an exaggeratedly nasal tone Rahmat would answer, also laughing, 'An elephant.'

The joke could not be termed particularly subtle, but nevertheless it kept both in splits— and the artless laughter of a middle-aged man and a child on an autumn morning brought me some joy too.

They had another ritual exchange. Rahmat would tell Mini, 'Khnokhi, tomi sasurbaari kakhanu jaabena.' Little girl, you must never get married and go to your father-in-law's house.

Most girls from traditional Bengali families would be familiar with the word shoshurbaari almost from the time they were born, but because we were somewhat modern, we hadn't taught our daughter the meaning of the term. So, she did not know what to make of Rahmat's request, but because it was against her nature to be silent and unresponsive, she would fire a counter-question. 'Will you go there?'

Rahmat would brandish his enormous fist

against an imaginary father-in-law, and say, 'I will kill the sasur first.'

Imagining the terrible fate awaiting this unknown creature, Mini would laugh her head off.

———

It was the clear season of autumn. In ancient times, this was when kings set off to conquer other lands. I had never been anywhere outside Calcutta, but precisely for that reason my mind wandered all over the world. In the quiet corner of my room, I was like an eternal traveller, pining for places around the globe. My heart began to race as soon as another country was mentioned, the sight of a foreigner conjured up a vision of a cottage amidst rivers and mountains and forests, and thoughts of a joyful, free way of life captured my imagination.

But I was so retiring by nature that the very

notion of abandoning my corner and stepping out into the world made me have visions of the sky crashing down on my head. That was why my conversations with this man from Kabul, this Kabuliwallah, every morning by the desk in my tiny room served the purpose of travel for me. Rugged and inaccessible, the scorched, red-hued mountain ranges rose high on either side of the road, a laden caravan of camels winding along the narrow trail between them; turbaned traders and travellers, some of them on the backs of camels, some on foot, some with spears, others with old-fashioned flint guns…with a voice like the rumbling of clouds, the Kabuliwallah would recount tales from his homeland in broken Bengali, and these images would float past my eyes.

Mini's mother was perpetually jumpy, her mind alive with imaginary fears. The slightest noise on the streets would lead her to believe that all the inebriated individuals in the world were rushing towards our house, bent on making mischief. Despite all the years (not too many actually) she had lived on earth, she had still not rid herself of the conviction that the universe was populated only by thieves and robbers and drunkards and snakes and tigers and malaria and earthworms and cockroaches and white men all intent on striking terror into her heart.

She was not entirely free of doubt about Rahmat, the Kabuliwallah, requesting me repeatedly to keep an eye on him. When I attempted to laugh away her suspicions, she would ask me probing questions. 'Aren't children ever kidnapped? Don't they have slaves in Afghanistan? Is it entirely impossible for a gigantic Kabuliwallah to kidnap a small child?'

I had to acknowledge that it was not entirely impossible but unlikely. The capacity for trust was not the same in everyone, which was why my wife remained suspicious of the

Kabuliwallah. But I could not stop Rahmat from visiting our house for no fault of his.

Rahmat usually went home around the end of January every year. He would be very busy collecting his dues at this time. He had to go from house to house, but still he made it a point to visit Mini once a day. There did seem to be a conspiracy between them. If he could not visit in the morning, he made his way to our house in the evening. It was true that I experienced a sudden surge of fear at the sight of the large man in his loose shalwar and kurta, standing in a dark corner of the room with his bags. But when a laughing Mini ran up to him, saying, 'Kabuliwallah, Kabuliwallah,' and the simple banter of old was resumed between the two friends of unequal age, my heart was filled with delight once more.

I was correcting proofs one day in my tiny room. The cold had grown sharper; as winter was about to bid farewell, there was a severe chill. The morning sunshine filtering through the window warmed my feet; it was a most pleasant sensation. It was about eight o'clock—most of those who had ventured out for their morning constitutionals, their heads and throats wrapped in mufflers, were already back home. Suddenly, there was an uproar in the street.

Looking out of the window I saw two policemen frogmarching our Rahmat, bound with ropes, up the road, followed by a group of curious urchins. Rahmat's clothes were bloodstained, and one of the policemen held a dagger dripping with blood. Going out, I stopped the policemen to inquire what the matter was.

The story was related partly by a policeman and partly by Rahmat himself. One of our neighbours owed Rahmat some money for a shawl from Rampur. When he disclaimed the debt, an altercation broke out, in the course of which Rahmat had stabbed him with his dagger.

The Kabuliwallah was showering expletives on the liar when Mini emerged from the house, calling out, 'Kabuliwallah, Kabuliwallah.'

Rahmat's expression changed in an instant to a cheerful smile. Since there was no bag slung from his shoulder today, they could not have their usual discussion about its magical contents. Mini asked him directly, 'Will you go to your father-in-law's house?'

'That's exactly where I am going,' Rahmat smiled back at her.

When he saw Mini wasn't amused, he showed her his arms bound with rope. 'I would have killed the sasur, but my hands are tied.'

Rahmat was in jail for several years for causing grievous bodily harm.

We forgot him, more or less. Going about

our everyday routines it didn't even occur to us how difficult it must be for a man used to roaming free in the mountains to cope with years of imprisonment.

Even Mini's father had to accept that his fickle-hearted daughter's behaviour was truly shameful. She effortlessly forgot her old friend, and struck up a new friendship with Nabi, who groomed horses. Then, as she grew older, male friends were replaced by girls her age. Now, we seldom saw each other any more.

Many years passed. Another autumn arrived. My Mini's wedding had been arranged. She would be married during the Durga Puja holidays. Along with the goddess from Kailash, the joy of my house would also depart for her husband's home, robbing her father's house of its light.

A beautiful morning had dawned. After the monsoon, the freshly-rinsed autumn sunlight had taken on the colour of pure molten gold.

Its glow washed over the crumbling houses of exposed brick in the neighbourhood, making them exquisitely beautiful.

The shehnai had begun playing in my house before the night had ended. Its notes were like the sound of my heart weeping. The plaintive melody of Bhairavi was spreading the imminent pain of parting all over the world. My Mini was to be married today.

There had been a great to-do since the morning, with crowds of people going in and out of the house. In the courtyard a marquee was being set up with bamboo posts; the clinking of chandeliers being hung up in the rooms and the veranda could be heard. It was very noisy.

I was going over the accounts in my room when Rahmat appeared and saluted me.

I did not recognize him at first. He had neither his bags nor his long hair—his body was not as strapping as it once used to be. It was his smile that eventually told me who he was.

'Why, it's Rahmat,' I said. 'When did you get back?'

'I was released from jail yesterday evening,' he answered.

His reply made me uncomfortable. Until now, I had never seen a murderer in the flesh, his presence here made me shrink back. On this auspicious day, I wished he would go away.

I told him, 'There's something important going on at home, I am busy. You'd better go today.'

At this he made ready to leave at once, but when he had reached the door, he said hesitantly, 'Can't I meet Khnokhi?'

He probably thought that Mini had not changed. Perhaps he expected her to come running up as before, chanting, 'Kabuliwallah, Kabuliwallah,' as she always had. To honour the old friendship he had even gone to the trouble of collecting a box of grapes and some nuts

and raisins wrapped in paper from a fellow
Afghan as he no longer had his own sack of
goods to sell.

'There are some ceremonies at home today,'
I told him, 'meeting Mini is impossible.'

He looked very disappointed. He looked at
me wordlessly for a few moments, then said,
'Salaam, Babu,' and left.

No sooner had he left than I felt bad and
was considering calling him back when I found
him returning of his own accord.

Coming up to me, he said, 'I have some
grapes and nuts and raisins for Khnokhi, please
give them to her.'

As I was about to pay for them, he caught
hold of my hand firmly and said, 'Please don't
pay me. You have always been so kind, I will
never forget your kindness....

'I have a daughter back home just like yours,
Babu. It was thinking of her that I brought
some fruit for Khnokhi; this isn't business.'

Putting his hand inside his long, loose shalwar, he pulled out a dirty piece of paper. Unfolding it carefully, he spread it out on my desk for me. It had the print of a tiny pair of hands. Not a photograph, not an oil painting, just some lampblack smeared on the palms to make a print on paper. Rahmat travelled to Calcutta's streets every year to sell his dry fruits, holding this remembrance of his daughter close to his breast—as though the touch of those tiny tender hands comforted the heart inside his broad chest, a heart wracked by the pain of separation.

Tears sprang to my eyes. I forgot that he was a seller of dry fruits from Kabul and I, a member of a Kulin Bengali family. I realized that he was a father, just as I was. The handprint of his little Parbati from his home in the mountains reminded me of Mini.

I sent for my daughter at once. They raised objections in the ladies' chambers, but I paid no attention. Mini appeared shyly in my room, dressed as a bride in her red wedding garb.

The Kabuliwallah was taken aback when he saw her. Unable to revive their old banter, he said nothing for a while. Finally, he said with a smile, 'Khnokhi, tomi sasurbaari jaabis?'

Mini knew now what the words meant, and she could not respond as before. Blushing at Rahmat's question, she stood with her face averted. I remembered the day Mini and the Kabuliwallah had met for the first time, and felt a twinge of sadness.

After Mini left, Rahmat slumped to the floor with a sigh. He had suddenly realized that his own daughter must have grown up and that he would have to get to know her all over again—she would no longer be the way he remembered her. Who knew what might have happened to her over these past eight years? The shehnai kept playing in the calming sunlight of the autumn morning, but inside a house in a Calcutta lane all that Rahmat could see were the mountains and cold deserts of Afghanistan.

I gave him some money. 'Go back home to your daughter, Rahmat,' I told him. 'Let the happiness of your reunion with her be a blessing for my Mini.'

Giving Rahmat the money meant pruning one or two things from the celebrations. The electric lights display was not as lavish as I had wanted it to be, nor were the musical arrangements as elaborate as planned. The ladies as usual objected strongly but, for me, the festivities were brightened by the benediction of a father's love.

IDGAH

MUNSHI PREMCHAND

Translated from the Hindustani by Khushwant Singh

A full thirty days after Ramadan comes Eid. How wonderful and beautiful is the morning of Eid! The trees look greener, the fields more festive, the sky has a lovely pink glow. Look at the sun! It comes up brighter and more dazzling than before to wish the world a very happy Eid. The village is agog with excitement. Everyone is up early to go to the Idgah mosque. One finds a button missing from his shirt and is hurrying to his neighbour's house for thread and needle. Another finds that the leather of his shoes has become hard and is running to the oil-press for oil to grease it.

They are dumping fodder before their oxen because by the time they get back from the Idgah it may be late afternoon. It is a good three miles from the village. There will also be hundreds of people to greet and chat with; they would certainly not be finished before midday.

The boys are more excited than the others. Some of them kept only one fast—and that only till noon. Some didn't even do that. But no one can deny them the joy of going to the Idgah. Fasting is for the grown-ups and the aged. For the boys it is only the day of Eid. They have been talking about it all the time. At long last the day has come. And now they are impatient with people for not hurrying up. They have no concern with things that have to be done. They are not bothered whether or not there is enough milk and sugar for the vermicelli pudding. All they want is to eat the pudding. They have no idea why Abbajan is out of breath, running to the house of Chaudhry Karim Ali. They don't know that if the Chaudhry were to change his mind, he could turn the festive day of Eid into a day of mourning. Their pockets bulge with coins like the stomach of the pot-bellied Kubera, the Hindu God of Wealth. They are forever taking the treasure out of their pockets, counting and recounting it before putting it back. Mahmood counts 'One, two, ten, twelve'—he has twelve paise. Mohsin has 'One, two, three, eight, nine, fifteen' paise. Out of this countless hoard they will buy countless things—toys, sweets, paper-pipes, rubber balls—and much else.

The happiest of the boys is Hamid. He is only four, poorly dressed, thin and famished-looking. His father died last year of cholera. Then his mother wasted away and, without anyone finding out what had ailed her, she also died. Now Hamid sleeps in Granny Ameena's lap and is as happy as a lark. She tells him that his father has gone to earn money and will return with sack loads of silver. And that his mother has gone to Allah to get lovely gifts for him. This makes Hamid very happy. It is great to live on hope; for a child there is nothing like hope. A child's imagination can turn a mustard seed into a mountain. Hamid has no shoes on his feet; the cap on his head is soiled and tattered; its gold thread has turned black. Nevertheless, Hamid is happy. He knows that when his father comes back with sacks full of silver and his mother with gifts from Allah, he will be able to fulfil all his heart's desires. Then he will have more than Mahmood, Mohsin, Noorey, and Sammi.

In her hovel the unfortunate Ameena sheds bitter tears. It is Eid and she does not have even a handful of grain. If only her Abid were there, it would have been a different kind of Eid!

Hamid goes to his grandmother and says, 'Granny, don't you fret over me! I will be the first to get back. Don't worry!'

Ameena is sad. Other boys are going out with their fathers. She is the only 'father' Hamid has. How can she let him go to the fair all by himself? What if he gets lost in the crowd? No, she must not lose her precious little soul! How can he walk three miles? He doesn't even have a pair of shoes. He will get blisters on his feet. If she went along with him, she could pick him up now and then. But then who would be there to cook the vermicelli? If only she had the money, she could have bought the ingredients on the way back and quickly made the pudding. In the village it would take her many hours to get everything. The only way out was to ask someone for them.

The villagers leave in one party. With the boys is Hamid. They run on ahead of the elders and wait for them under a tree. Why do the oldies drag their feet? And Hamid is like one with wings on his feet. How could anyone think he would get tired?

They reach the suburbs of the town. On both sides of the road are mansions of the rich, enclosed all around by thick, high walls. In the gardens, mango and litchi trees are laden with fruit. A boy hurls a stone at a mango tree. The gardener rushes out screaming abuses at them. By then the boys are a furlong out of his reach and roaring with laughter. What a silly ass they make of the gardener!

Then come big buildings: the law courts, the college, and the club. How many boys would there be in this big college? No, sir, they are not all boys! Some are grown-up men. They sport enormous moustaches.

What are such grown-up men going on studying for? How long will they go on doing so? What will they do with all their knowledge? There are only two or three grown-up boys in Hamid's school. Absolute duds they are too! They get a thrashing every day because they do not work at all. These college fellows must be the same type—why else should they be there! And the Masonic Lodge. They perform magic there. It is rumoured that they make human skulls move about and do other kinds of weird things. No wonder they don't let in outsiders! And the white folk play games in the evenings. Grown-up men, men with moustaches and beards playing games! And not only they, but even their memsahibs! That's the honest truth! You give my granny that something they call a racket; she wouldn't know how to hold it. And if she tried to wave it about, she would collapse.

Mahmood says, 'My mother's hands would shake; I swear by Allah they would!'

Mohsin says, 'Mine can grind maunds of grain. Her hand would never shake holding a miserable racket. She draws hundreds of pitchers full of water from the well every day. My buffalo drinks up five pitchers. If a memsahib had to draw one pitcher, she would go blue in the face.'

Mahmood interrupts, 'But your mother couldn't run and leap about, could she?'

'That's right,' replies Mohsin, 'she couldn't leap or jump. But one day our cow got loose and began grazing in the Chaudhry's fields. My mother ran so fast after it that I couldn't catch up with her. Honest to God, I could not!'

So they proceed to the stores of the sweetmeat vendors. All so gaily decorated! Who can eat all these delicacies? Just look! Every store has them piled up in mountainous heaps. They say that after nightfall jinns come and buy up everything. 'My abba says that at midnight there is a jinn at every stall. He has all that remains weighed and pays in real rupees, just the sort of rupees we have,' says Mohsin.

Hamid is not convinced. 'Where would the jinns come by rupees?'

'Jinns are never short of money,' replies

Mohsin. 'They can get into any treasury they want. Mister, don't you know, no iron bars can stop them? They have all the diamonds and rubies they want. If they are pleased with someone, they will give him baskets full of diamonds. They are here one moment and five minutes later they can be in Calcutta.'

Hamid asks again, 'Are these jinns very big?'

'Each one is as big as the sky,' asserts Mohsin. 'He has his feet on the ground, his head touches the sky. But if he so wanted, he could get into a tiny brass pot.'

'How do people make jinns happy?' asks Hamid. 'If anyone taught me the secret, I would make at least one jinn happy with me.'

'I do not know,' replies Mohsin, 'but the Chaudhry sahib has a lot of jinns under his control. If anything is stolen, he can trace it and even tell you the name of the thief. Jinns tell him everything that is going on in the world.'

Hamid understands how Chaudhry sahib

has come by his wealth and why people hold him in so much respect.

It begins to get crowded. Parties heading for the Idgah are coming into town from different sides—each one dressed better than the other. Some in tongas and ekkas; some in motor cars. All wearing perfume; all bursting with excitement.

The small party of village rustics is not bothered about the poor show they make. They are a calm, contented lot.

For village children everything in the town is strange. Whatever catches their eye, they stand and gape at it with wonder. Cars hoot frantically to get them out of the way, but they couldn't care less. Hamid is nearly run over by a car.

At long last the Idgah comes in, view. Above it are massive tamarind trees casting their shade on the cemented floor on which carpets have been spread. And there are row upon row of worshippers as far as the eye can see, spilling well beyond the mosque courtyard. Newcomers line themselves behind the others. Here neither wealth nor status matters because in the eyes of Islam all men are equal. Our villagers wash their hands and feet and make their own line behind the others. What a beautiful, heart-moving sight it is! What perfect coordination of movements! A hundred thousand heads bow together in prayer! And then all together they stand erect; bow down and sit on their knees! Many times they repeat these movements—exactly as if a hundred thousand electric bulbs were switched on and off at the same time again and again. What a wonderful spectacle it is!

The prayer is over. Men embrace each other. They descend on the sweet and toy vendors' stores like an army moving to an assault. In this matter the grown-up rustic is no less eager than the boys. Look, here is a swing! Pay a paisa and enjoy riding up to the heavens and then plummeting down to the earth. And here is the roundabout strung with wooden elephants, horses, and camels! Pay one paisa and have twenty-five rounds of fun. Mahmood and Mohsin and Noorey and other boys mount the horses and camels.

Hamid watches them from a distance. All he has are three paise. He couldn't afford to part with a third of his treasure for a few miserable rounds.

They've finished with the roundabouts; now it is time for the toys. There is a row of stalls on one side with all kinds of toys: soldiers and milkmaids, kings and ministers, water-carriers and washerwomen and holy men. Splendid display! How lifelike! All they need are tongues to speak. Mahmood buys a policeman in khaki with a red turban on his head and a gun on his shoulder. Looks as if he is marching in a parade. Mohsin likes the water-carrier with his back bent under the weight of the water bag. He holds the handle of the bag in one hand

and looks pleased with himself. Perhaps he is singing. It seems as if the water is about to pour out of the bag. Noorey has fallen for the lawyer. What an expression of learning he has on his face! A black gown over a long white coat with a gold watch chain going into a pocket, a fat volume of some law book in his hand. He looks like he has just finished arguing a case in a court of law.

These toys cost two paise each. All Hamid has are three paise; how can he afford to buy such expensive toys? If they dropped out of his hand, they would be smashed to bits. If a drop of water fell on them, the paint would run. What would he do with toys like these? They'd be of no use to him.

Mohsin says, 'My water-carrier will sprinkle water every day, morning and evening.'

Mahmood says, 'My policeman will guard my house. If a thief comes near, he will shoot him with his gun.'

Noorey says, 'My lawyer will fight my cases.'

Sammi says, 'My washerwoman will wash my clothes every day.'

Hamid pooh-poohs their toys—they're made of clay—one fall and they'll break into pieces. But his eyes look at them hungrily and he wishes he could hold them in his hands for just a moment or two. His hands stretch without his wanting to stretch them. But young boys are not givers, particularly when it is something new. Poor Hamid doesn't get to touch the toys.

After the toys, it is sweets. Someone buys sesame seed candy, others gulab jamuns or halwa. They smack their lips with relish. Only Hamid is left out. The luckless boy has at least three paise; why doesn't he also buy something to eat? He looks with hungry eyes at the others.

Mohsin says, 'Hamid, take this sesame candy, it smells good.'

Hamid suspects it is a cruel joke; he knows

Mohsin doesn't have so big a heart. But despite knowing this Hamid goes to Mohsin. Mohsin takes a piece out of his leaf-wrap and holds it towards Hamid. Hamid stretches out his hand. Mohsin puts the candy in his own mouth. Mahmood, Noorey, and Sammi clap their hands with glee and have a jolly good laugh. Hamid is crestfallen.

Mohsin says, 'This time I will let you have it. I swear by Allah! I will give it to you. Come and take it.'

Hamid replies, 'You keep your sweets. Don't I have money?'

'All you have are three paise,' says Sammi. 'What can you buy for three paise?'

Mahmood says, 'Mohsin is a rascal. Hamid, you come to me and I will give you gulab jamun.'

Hamid replies, 'What is there to rave about sweets? Books are full of bad things about eating sweets.'

'In your heart you must be saying, "If I could get it, I would eat it,"' says Mohsin. 'Why don't you take the money out of your pocket?'

'I know what this clever fellow is up to,' says Mahmood. 'When we've spent all our money, he will buy sweets and tease us.'

After the sweet vendors there are a few hardware stores and shops of real and artificial jewellery. There is nothing there to attract the boys' attention. So, they go ahead, all of them except Hamid who stops to see a pile of tongs. It occurs to him that his granny does not have a pair of tongs. Each time she bakes chapatis, the iron plate burns her hands. If he were to buy her a pair of tongs, she would be very pleased. She would never burn her fingers; it would be a useful thing to have in the house. What use are toys? They are a waste of money. You can have some fun with them but only for a very short time. Then you forget all about them.

Hamid's friends have gone ahead. They are at a stall drinking sherbet. How selfish they are! They bought so many sweets but did not give him one. And then they want him to play with them; they want him to do odd jobs for them. Now if any of them asked him to do something, he would tell them, 'Go suck your lollipop, it will burn your mouth; it will give you a rash of pimples and boils; your tongue will always crave for sweets; you will have to steal money to buy them and get a thrashing in the bargain. It's all written in books. Nothing will happen to my tongs. No sooner my granny sees my pair of tongs she will run up to take it from me and say, "My child has brought me a pair of tongs," and shower me with a thousand blessings. She will show it off to the neighbour womenfolk. Soon the whole village will be saying, "Hamid has brought his granny a pair of tongs, how nice he is!" No one will bless the other boys for the toys they have got for themselves. Blessings of elders are heard in the court of Allah and are immediately acted on. Because I have no money, Mohsin and Mahmood adopt such airs towards me. I will teach them a lesson. Let them play with their toys and eat all the sweets they can. I will not play with toys. I will not stand any nonsense from anyone. And one day my father will return. And also my mother. Then I will ask these chaps, "Do you want any toys? How many?" I will give each one a basket full of toys and teach them how to treat friends. I am not the sort who buys a paisa worth of lollipops to tease others by sucking them myself. I know they will laugh and say Hamid has brought a pair of tongs. They can go to the Devil!'

Hamid asks the shopkeeper, 'How much for this pair of tongs?'

The shopkeeper looks at him and seeing

no older person with him replies, 'It's not for you.'

'Is it for sale or not?'

'Why should it not be for sale? Why else should I have bothered to bring it here?'

'Then why don't you tell me how much it is!'

'It will cost you six paise.'

Hamid's heart sinks. 'Let me have the correct price.'

'All right, it will be five paise, bottom price. Take it or leave it.' Hamid steels his heart and says, 'Will you give it to me for three?' And proceeds to walk away lest the shopkeeper scream at him. But the shopkeeper does not scream. On the contrary, he calls Hamid back and gives him the pair of tongs. Hamid carries it on his shoulder as if it were a gun and struts up proudly to show it to his friends. Let us hear what they have to say.

Mohsin laughs and says, 'Are you crazy?

What will you do with the tongs?' Hamid flings the tongs on the ground and replies, 'Try and throw your water-carrier on the ground. Every bone in his body will break.'

Mahmood says, 'Are these tongs some kind of toy?'

'Why not?' retorts Hamid. 'Place them across your shoulders and it is a gun; wield them in your hands and it is like the tongs carried by singing mendicants—they can make the same clanging as a pair of cymbals. One smack and they will reduce all your toys to dust. And much as your toys may try, they cannot bend a hair on the head of my tongs. My tongs are like a brave tiger.'

Sammi who had bought a small tambourine asks, 'Will you exchange them for my tambourine? It is worth eight paise.'

Hamid pretends not to look at the tambourine. 'My tongs, if they wanted to, could tear out the bowels of your tambourine. All it has is a leather skin and all it can say is *dhub, dhub.* A drop of water could silence it forever. My brave pair of tongs can weather water and storms without budging an inch.'

The pair of tongs wins everyone over to its side. But now no one has any money left and the fairground has been left far behind. It is well past 9 a.m. and the sun is getting hotter every minute. Everyone is in a hurry to get home. Even if they talked their fathers into it, they could not get the tongs. This Hamid is a bit of a rascal. He saved up his money for the tongs.

The boys divide into two factions. Mohsin, Mahmood, Sammi, and Noorey on the one side, and Hamid by himself on the other. They are engaged in hot argument. Sammi has defected to the other side. But Mohsin, Mahmood, and Noorey, though they are a year or two older than Hamid, are reluctant to take him on in debate. Right is on Hamid's side.

Also it's moral force on the one side, clay on the other. Hamid has iron, now calling itself steel, unconquerable and lethal. If a tiger were to spring on them, the water-carrier would be out of his wits; Mister Constable would drop his clay gun and take to his heels; the lawyer would hide his face in his gown, lie down on the ground, and wail as if his mother's mother had died. But the tongs, the pair of tongs, Champion of India, would leap and grab the tiger by its neck and gouge out its eyes.

Mohsin puts all he has in his plea, 'But they cannot go and fetch water, can they?'

Hamid raises the tongs and replies, 'One angry word of command from my tongs and your water-carrier will hasten to fetch the water and sprinkle it at any doorstep he is ordered to.'

Mohsin has no answer. Mahmood comes to his rescue. 'If we are caught, we are caught. We will have to do the rounds of the law courts in chains. Then we will be at the lawyer's feet asking for help.'

Hamid has no answer to this powerful argument. He asks, 'Who will come to arrest us?'

Noorey puffs out his chest and replies, 'This policeman with the gun.'

Hamid makes a face and says with scorn, 'This wretch has come to arrest the Champion of India! Okay, let's have it out over a bout of wrestling; far from catching them, he will be scared to look my tongs in the face.'

Mohsin thinks of another ploy. 'Your tongs' face will burn in the fire every day.' He is sure that this will leave Hamid speechless. That is not so. Pat comes Hamid with the retort, 'Mister, it is only the brave who can jump into a fire. Your miserable lawyers, policemen, and water-carriers will run like frightened women into their homes. Only this Champion of India can perform this feat of leaping into the fire.'

Mahmood has one more try, 'The lawyer will have chairs to sit on and tables for his things. Your tongs will only have the kitchen floor to lie on.'

Hamid cannot think of an appropriate retort so he says whatever comes into his mind, 'The tongs won't stay in the kitchen. When your lawyer sits on his chair, my tongs will knock him down to the ground.'

It does not make sense but our three heroes are utterly squashed—almost as if a champion kite had been brought down from the heavens to the earth by a cheap, miserable paper imitation. Thus, Hamid wins the field. His tongs are the Champion of India. Neither Mohsin nor Mahmood, neither Noorey nor Sammi—nor anyone else can dispute the fact.

The respect that a victor commands from the vanquished is paid to Hamid. The others have spent between twelve to sixteen paise each and bought nothing worthwhile. Hamid's three-paise worth has carried the day. And no one can deny that toys are unreliable things: they break, while Hamid's tongs will remain as they are for years.

The boys begin to make terms of peace. Mohsin says, 'Give me your tongs for a while, you can have my water-carrier for the same time.'

Both Mahmood and Noorey similarly offer their toys. Hamid has no hesitation in agreeing to these terms. The tongs pass from one hand to another; and the toys are in turn handed to Hamid. How lovely they are!

Hamid tries to wipe the tears of his defeated adversaries. 'I was simply pulling your leg, honestly I was. How can these tongs made of iron compare with your toys?' It seems that one or the other will call Hamid's bluff. But Mohsin's party are not solaced. The tongs have won the day and no amount of water can wash away their stamp of authority. Mohsin says, 'No one will bless us for these toys.'

Mahmood adds, 'You talk of blessings! We may get a thrashing instead. My amma is bound to say, "Are these earthen toys all that you could find at the fair?"'

Hamid has to concede that no mother will be as pleased with the toys as his granny will be when she sees the tongs. All he had was three paise and he has no reason to regret the way he has spent them. And now his tongs are the Champion of India and King of Toys.

By eleven, the village was again agog with excitement. All those who had gone to the fair were back at home. Mohsin's little sister ran up, wrenched the water-carrier out of his hands, and began to dance with joy. Mister Water-carrier slipped out of her hand, fell on the ground, and went to paradise. The brother and sister began to fight; and both had lots to cry about. Their mother lost her temper because of the racket they were making and gave each two resounding slaps.

Noorey's lawyer met an end befitting his grand status. A lawyer could not sit on the ground. He had to keep his dignity in mind. Two nails were driven into the wall, a plank put on them and a carpet of paper spread on the plank. The honourable counsel was seated like a king on his throne. Noorey began to wave a fan over him. He knew that in the law courts there were khus curtains and electric fans. So the least he could do was to provide a hand fan, otherwise the hot legal arguments might affect his lawyer's brains. Noorey was waving his fan made of bamboo leaf. We do not know whether it was the breeze or the fan or something else that brought the honourable counsel down from his high pedestal to the depths of hell and reduced his gown to mingle with the dust of which it was made. There was much beating of breasts and the lawyer's bier was dumped on a dung heap.

Mahmood's policeman remained. He was immediately put on duty to guard the village. But this police constable was no ordinary mortal who could walk on his own two feet. He had to be provided a palanquin. This was a basket lined with tatters of discarded clothes of red colour for the policeman to recline on in comfort. Mahmood picked up the basket and started on his rounds. His two younger brothers followed him lisping, 'Shleepers, keep awake!' But night has to be dark; Mahmood stumbled, the basket slipped out of his hand. Mr Constable, with his gun, crashed to the ground. He was short of one leg.

Mahmood, being a bit of a doctor, knew of an ointment which could quickly rejoin broken limbs. All it needed was the milk of a banyan sapling. The milk was brought and the broken leg reassembled.

But no sooner was the constable put on his feet than the leg gave way. One leg was of no use because now he could neither walk nor sit. Mahmood became a surgeon and cut the other leg to the size of the broken one so the chap could at least sit in comfort.

The constable was made into a holy man; he could sit in one place and guard the village. And sometimes he was like the image of the deity. The plume on his turban was scraped off and you could make as many changes in his appearance as you liked. And sometimes he was used for nothing better than weighing things down.

Now let's hear what happened to our friend Hamid. As soon as she heard his voice, Granny Ameena ran out of the house, picked him up, and kissed him. Suddenly she noticed the tongs in his hand. 'Where did you find these tongs?'

'I bought them.'

'How much did you pay for them?'

'Three paise.'

Granny Ameena beat her breast. 'You are a

stupid child! It is almost noon and you haven't had anything to eat or drink. And what do you buy—tongs! Couldn't you find anything better in the fair than this pair of iron tongs?'

Hamid replied in injured tones, 'You burn your fingers on the iron plate. That is why I bought them.'

The old woman's temper suddenly changed to love—not the kind of calculated love, which wastes away in spoken words. This love was mute, solid, and steeped with tenderness. What a selfless child! What concern for others! What a big heart! How he must have suffered seeing other boys buying toys and gobbling sweets! How was he able to suppress his own feelings! Even at the fair he thought of his old grandmother. Granny Ameena's heart was too full for words.

And the strangest thing happened—stranger than the part played by the tongs was the role of Hamid the child playing Hamid the old man. And old Granny Ameena became Ameena the little girl. She broke down. She spread her apron and beseeched Allah's blessings for her grandchild. Big tears fell from her eyes. How was Hamid to understand what was going on inside her!

PORTRAIT OF A LADY
KHUSHWANT SINGH

My grandmother, like everybody's grandmother, was an old woman. She had been old and wrinkled for the twenty years that I had known her. People said that she had once been young and pretty and had even had a husband, but that was hard to believe. My grandfather's portrait hung above the mantelpiece in the drawing room. He wore a big turban and loose-fitting clothes. His long white beard covered the best part of his chest and he looked at least a hundred years old. He did not look the sort of person who would have a wife or children. He looked as if he could only have lots and lots of grandchildren. As for my grandmother being young and pretty, the thought was almost revolting. She often told us of the games she used to play as a child. That seemed quite absurd and undignified on her part and we treated them like the fables of the prophets she used to tell us.

She had always been short and fat and slightly bent. Her face was a criss-cross of wrinkles running from everywhere to everywhere. No, we were certain she had always been as we had known her. Old, so terribly old that she could not have grown older, and had stayed at the same age for twenty years. She could never have been pretty; but she was always beautiful. She hobbled about the house in spotless white, with one hand resting on her waist to balance her stoop and the other telling the beads of her rosary. Her silver locks were scattered untidily over her pale, puckered face, and her lips constantly moved in inaudible prayer. Yes, she was beautiful. She was like the winter landscape in the mountains, an expanse of pure white serenity breathing peace and contentment.

My grandmother and I were good friends. My parents left me with her when they went to live in the city and we were constantly together. She used to wake me up in the morning and get me ready for school. She said her morning prayer in a monotonous sing-song while she bathed and dressed me in the hope that I would listen and get to know it by heart. I listened because I loved her voice but never bothered to learn it. Then she would fetch my wooden slate which she had already washed and plastered with yellow chalk, a tiny earthen ink pot and a reed pen, tie them all in a bundle and hand it to me. After a breakfast of a thick, stale chapati with a little butter and sugar spread on it, we went to school. She carried several stale chapatis with her for the village dogs.

My grandmother always went to school

with me because the school was attached to the temple. The priest taught us the alphabet and the morning prayer. While the children sat in rows on either side of the veranda singing the alphabet or the prayer in a chorus, my grandmother sat inside reading the scriptures. When we had both finished, we would walk back together. This time the village dogs would meet us at the temple door. They followed us to our home, growling and fighting each other for the chapatis we threw to them.

When my parents were comfortably settled in the city, they sent for us. That was a turning point in our friendship. Although we shared the same room, my grandmother no longer came to school with me. I used to go to an English school in a motor bus. There were no dogs in the streets and she took to feeding sparrows in the courtyard of our city house.

As the years rolled by, we saw less of each other. For some time, she continued to wake me up and get me ready for school. When I came back, she would ask me what the teacher had taught me. I would tell her English words and little things of Western science and learning, the law of gravity, Archimedes' principle, the world being round, etc. This made her unhappy. She could not help me with my lessons. She did not believe in the things they taught at the English school and was distressed that there was no teaching about God and the scriptures. One day I announced that we were being given music lessons. She was very disturbed. To her music had lewd associations. It was the monopoly of harlots and beggars and not meant for gentlefolk. She rarely talked to me after that.

When I went up to university, I was given a room of my own. The common link of friendship was snapped. My grandmother accepted her seclusion with resignation. She rarely left her spinning wheel to talk to anyone.

From sunrise to sunset she sat by her wheel, spinning and reciting prayers. Only in the afternoon she relaxed for a while to feed the sparrows. While she sat in the veranda breaking the bread into little bits, hundreds of little birds collected around her, creating a veritable bedlam of chirrupings. Some came and perched on her legs, others on her shoulders. Some even sat on her head. She smiled but never shooed them away. It used to be the happiest half hour of the day for her.

When I decided to go abroad for further studies, I was sure my grandmother would be upset. I would be away for five years and, at her age, one could never tell. But my grandmother could. She was not even sentimental. She came to leave me at the railway station but did not talk or show any emotion. Her lips moved in prayer, her mind was lost in prayer. Her fingers were busy telling the beads of her rosary. Silently she kissed my forehead, and when I left, I cherished the moist imprint as perhaps the last sign of physical contact between us.

But that was not so. After five years I came back home and was met by her at the station. She did not look a day older. She still had no time for words, and while she clasped me in her arms, I could hear her reciting her prayer. Even on the first day of my arrival, her happiest moments were with her sparrows, whom she fed longer and with frivolous rebukes.

In the evening a change came over her. She did not pray. She collected the women of the neighbourhood, got an old drum and started to sing. For several hours she thumped the sagging skins of the dilapidated drum and sang of the homecoming of warriors. We had to persuade her to stop to avoid overstraining. That was the first time since I had known her that she did not pray.

The next morning, she was taken ill. It was a mild fever and the doctor told us that it would go. But my grandmother thought differently. She told us that her end was near. She said that, since only a few hours before the close of the last chapter of her life she had omitted to pray, she was not going to waste any more time talking to us.

We protested. But she ignored our protests. She lay peacefully in bed, praying and telling her beads. Even before we could suspect, her lips stopped moving and the rosary fell from her lifeless fingers. A peaceful pallor spread on her face and we knew that she was dead.

We lifted her off the bed and, as is customary, laid her on the ground and covered her with a red shroud. After a few hours of mourning, we left her alone to make arrangements for her funeral.

In the evening, we went to her room with a crude stretcher to take her to be cremated. The sun was setting and had lit her room and veranda with a blaze of golden light. We stopped halfway in the courtyard. All over the veranda and in her room right up to where she lay dead and stiff, wrapped in the red shroud, thousands of sparrows sat scattered on the floor. There was no chirping. We felt sorry for the birds and my mother fetched some bread for them. She broke it into little crumbs, the way my grandmother used to, and threw it to them. The sparrows took no notice of the bread. When we carried my grandmother's corpse off, they flew away quietly. Next morning, the sweeper swept the breadcrumbs into the dustbin.

THE WHY-WHY GIRL
MAHASWETA DEVI

'But why?'

The question came from a small girl, about ten years old. She was chasing a large snake.

I* ran after her, grabbed her plait and held her back, shouting, 'No, Moyna, don't!'

'Why shouldn't I?' she asked.

'It's not a grass snake or a rat snake, it's a cobra,' I replied.

'Why shouldn't I catch a cobra?'

'Why should you?'

'We eat snakes, you know,' Moyna said. 'The

---

*The 'I' in the story is Mahasweta Devi herself. She worked a lot with tribal groups.

head you chop off, the skin you sell, the meat you cook.'

'Yes, but don't do it this time,' I said.

'I will, I will.'

'No, child!'

'But why?'

I dragged Moyna back to the Samiti office,[*] where I worked. Her mother, Khiri, was there, weaving a basket. The Samiti was a place where people could come to learn to read and write, or simply sing and dance together.

'Come,' I said to Moyna. 'Come and rest for a little while.'

'Why?'

'Aren't you tired?' I asked. Moyna shook her head vigorously.

'Who will bring the goats home? And collect firewood and fetch water and lay traps for the birds?' came the questions, one after another.

---

[*]Samiti is the group Mahasweta Devi worked with, along with the local tribal people.

'Moyna, don't forget to thank the Babu for the rice he sent us,' said Khiri.

'Why should I?' Moyna said. 'Don't I sweep the cowshed and do a thousand jobs for him? Does he ever thank me? Why should I?' Saying this, Moyna ran off.

Khiri sighed and shook her head. 'Never seen a child like this. All she keeps saying is "Why". No wonder the postmaster calls her Why-Why Girl!'

'I like her,' I said.

'But she's very obstinate,' Khiri retorted. 'Just won't give in.'

Moyna was a Shabar. The Shabars were a poor tribal group, and they owned no land. But nobody complained. Only Moyna's questions went on and on.

'Why do I have to walk so far to the river to fetch water? Why do we live in a leaf hut? Why can't we eat rice twice a day?'

Moyna tended the goats of the village

landlords or babus, but she was neither humble nor grateful. She did her work and came home in the evening.

'Why should I eat their leftovers?' she would say. 'I will cook a delicious meal with green leaves and rice and crabs and chilli powder and eat with my family.'

The Shabars did not usually send their daughters to work. But Moyna's mother had a bad leg and so couldn't walk properly. Her father had gone off to faraway Jamshedpur in search of work and her brother, Goro, went to the forest every day to collect firewood. So Moyna had to work.

That October, I stayed in the village for a month. One morning, Moyna declared that she would move in with me.

'No,' said Khiri.

'Why not? It's a big hut. How much space does one old woman need?' Moyna said, referring to me, of course.

'What about going to work?' her mother asked.

'I'll go, but I'll come here after work,' Moyna said firmly.

And she came, with one change of clothes and a baby mongoose. 'It eats very little and chases away the bad snakes,' she said. 'The good snakes I catch and give to Mother. She makes lovely snake curry. I'll bring some for you.'

Our Samiti teacher, Malati, said to me, 'She'll exhaust you with her whys!'

What a time I had with Moyna!

'Why do I have to graze the babus' goats? Their boys can do it.'

'Why can't fish speak?'

'Why do stars look so small if many of them are bigger than the sun?'

One night she asked me, 'Why do you read books before you go to sleep?'

'Because books have the answers to your whys!' I replied. And for once, Moyna was silent.

She tidied the room, watered the flowering tree, and fed fish to the mongoose. Then she came up to me and said, 'I will learn to read and find the answers to my questions.'

When Moyna grazed the goats, she told the other children all that she had learned from me.

'Many stars are bigger than the sun. But they live far away, so they look small. The sun is nearer, so it looks bigger. The fish do not speak like us. They have a fish language, which is silent. The earth is round, did you know that?'

When I returned to the village a year later, the first thing I heard was Moyna's voice. 'Why is the school closed?' she challenged Malati as she entered the Samiti's school, dragging along a bleating goat.

'What do you mean, why?' asked Malati.

'Why shouldn't I study too?' asked Moyna.

'Who's stopping you?'

'But there's no class!'

'School is over for the day,' Malati pointed out.

'Why?'

'Because, Moyna, I take class from nine to eleven in the morning,' said Malati.

Moyna stamped her foot and said, 'Why can't you change the hours? I have to graze the goats in the morning. I can come only after eleven. If you don't teach me, how will I learn? I will tell the old lady'—me!—'that none of us, goatherds and cowherds, can come if the hours are not changed.'

Then she saw me and fled with her goat.

I went to Moyna's house in the evening. Nestling close to the kitchen fire, Moyna was telling her little sister and elder brother, 'You cut one tree and plant another two. You wash your hands before you eat, do you know why? You'll get stomach pain if you don't. You know nothing—do you know why? Because you don't attend classes at the Samiti.'

Who do you think was the first girl to be admitted to the village primary school?

Moyna.

Moyna is eighteen now. She teaches at the Samiti. If you pass by, you are sure to hear her impatient, demanding voice, 'Don't be lazy. Ask me questions. Ask me why mosquitoes should be destroyed, why the pole star is always in the north sky.'

And the other children too are learning to ask 'why'.

Moyna doesn't know I'm writing her story. If she did, she'd say, 'Writing about me? Why?'

THE BLUE UMBRELLA

RUSKIN BOND

I

'Neelu! Neelu' cried Binya.

She scrambled barefoot over the rocks, ran over the short summer grass, up and over the brow of the hill, all the time calling 'Neelu, Neelu!' Neelu—Blue—was the name of the blue-grey cow. The other cow, which was white, was called Gori, meaning Fair One. They were fond of wandering off on their own, down to the stream or into the pine forest, and sometimes they came back by themselves and sometimes they stayed away— almost deliberately, it seemed to Binya.

If the cows didn't come home at the right

time, Binya would be sent to fetch them. Sometimes her brother, Bijju, went with her, but these days he was busy preparing for his exams and didn't have time to help with the cows.

Binya liked being on her own, and sometimes she allowed the cows to lead her into some distant valley, and then they would all be late coming home. The cows preferred having Binya with them, because she let them wander. Bijju pulled them by their tails if they went too far.

Binya belonged to the mountains, to this part of the Himalaya known as Garhwal. Dark forests and lonely hilltops held no terrors for her. It was only when she was in the market town, jostled by the crowds in the bazaar, that she felt rather nervous and lost. The town, five miles from the village, was also a pleasure resort for tourists from all over India.

Binya was probably ten. She may have

been nine or even eleven, she couldn't be sure because no one in the village kept birthdays; but her mother told her she'd been born during a winter when the snow had come up to the windows, and that was just over ten years ago, wasn't it? Two years later, her father had died, but his passing had made no difference to their way of life. They had three tiny terraced fields on the side of the mountain, and they grew potatoes, onions, ginger, beans, mustard, and maize: not enough to sell in the town, but enough to live on.

Like most mountain girls, Binya was quite sturdy, fair of skin, with pink cheeks and dark eyes and her black hair tied in a pigtail. She wore pretty glass bangles on her wrists, and a necklace of glass beads. From the necklace hung a leopard's claw. It was a lucky charm, and Binya always wore it. Bijju had one, too, only his was attached to a string.

Binya's full name was Binyadevi, and Bijju's

real name was Vijay, but everyone called them Binya and Bijju. Binya was two years younger than her brother.

She had stopped calling for Neelu; she had heard the cowbells tinkling, and knew the cows hadn't gone far. Singing to herself, she walked over fallen pine needles into the forest glade on the spur of the hill. She heard voices, laughter, the clatter of plates and cups and, stepping through the trees, she came upon a party of picnickers.

They were holidaymakers from the plains. The women were dressed in bright saris, the men wore light summer shirts, and the children had pretty new clothes. Binya, standing in the shadows between the trees, went unnoticed; for some time she watched the picnickers, admiring their clothes, listening to their unfamiliar accents, and gazing rather hungrily at the sight of all their food. And then her gaze came to rest on a bright blue umbrella, a frilly thing for women, which lay open on the grass beside its owner.

Now Binya had seen umbrellas before, and her mother had a big black umbrella which nobody used any more because the field rats had eaten holes in it, but this was the first time Binya had seen such a small, dainty, colourful umbrella and she fell in love with it. The umbrella was like a flower, a great blue flower that had sprung up on the dry brown hillside.

She moved forward a few paces so that she could see the umbrella better. As she came out of the shadows into the sunlight, the picnickers saw her.

'Hello, look who's here!' exclaimed the older of the two women. 'A little village girl!'

'Isn't she pretty?' remarked the other. 'But how torn and dirty her clothes are!' It did not seem to bother them that Binya could hear and understand everything they said about her.

'They're very poor in the hills,' said one of the men.

'Then let's give her something to eat.' And the older woman beckoned to Binya to come closer.

Hesitantly, nervously, Binya approached the group.

Normally she would have turned and fled, but the attraction was the pretty blue umbrella. It had cast a spell over her, drawing her forward almost against her will.

'What's that on her neck?' asked the younger woman.

'A necklace of sorts.'

'It's a pendant—see, there's a claw hanging from it!' 'It's a tiger's claw,' said the man beside her. (He had never seen a tiger's claw.) 'A lucky charm. These people wear them to keep away evil spirits.' He looked to Binya for confirmation, but Binya said nothing.

'Oh, I want one too!' said the woman, who

was obviously his wife.

'You can't get them in shops.'

'Buy hers, then. Give her two or three rupees, she's sure to need the money.'

The man, looking slightly embarrassed but anxious to please his young wife, produced a two-rupee note and offered it to Binya, indicating that he wanted the pendant in exchange. Binya put her hand to the necklace, half afraid that the excited woman would snatch it away from her. Solemnly she shook her head.

The man then showed her a five-rupee note, but again Binya shook her head.

'How silly she is!' exclaimed the young woman.

'It may not be hers to sell,' said the man. 'But I'll try again. How much do you want— what can we give you?' And he waved his hand towards the picnic things scattered about on the grass.

Without any hesitation, Binya pointed to the

umbrella. 'My umbrella!' exclaimed the young woman. 'She wants my umbrella. What cheek!'

'Well, you want her pendant, don't you?'

'That's different.'

'Is it?'

The man and his wife were beginning to quarrel with each other.

'I'll ask her to go away,' said the older woman.

'We're making such fools of ourselves.'

'But I want the pendant!' cried the other, petulantly.

And then, on an impulse, she picked up the umbrella and held it out to Binya.

'Here, take the umbrella!'

Binya removed her necklace and held it out to the young woman, who immediately placed it around her own neck. Then Binya took the umbrella and held it up. It did not look so small in her hands; in fact, it was just the right size.

She had forgotten about the picnickers, who were busy examining the pendant. She turned the blue umbrella this way and that, looked through the bright blue silk at the pulsating sun, and then, still keeping it open, turned and disappeared into the forest glade.

II

Binya seldom closed the blue umbrella. Even when she had it in the house, she left it lying open in a corner of the room. Sometimes Bijju snapped it shut, complaining that it got in the way. She would open it again a little later. It wasn't beautiful when it was closed.

Whenever Binya went out—whether it was to graze the cows, or fetch water from the spring, or carry milk to the little tea shop on the Tehri road—she took the umbrella with her. That patch of sky-blue silk could always be seen on the hillside.

Old Ram Bharosa (Ram the Trustworthy)

kept the tea shop on the Tehri road. It was a dusty, unmetalled road. Once a day, the Tehri bus stopped near his shop and passengers got down to sip hot tea or drink a glass of curd. He kept a few bottles of Coca-Cola too, but as there was no ice, the bottles got hot in the sun and so were seldom opened. He also kept sweets and toffees, and when Binya or Bijju had a few coins to spare, they would spend them at the shop. It was only a mile from the village.

Ram Bharosa was astonished to see Binya's blue umbrella.

'What have you there, Binya?' he asked.

Binya gave the umbrella a twirl and smiled at Ram Bharosa. She was always ready with her smile, and would willingly have lent it to anyone who was feeling unhappy.

'That's a lady's umbrella,' said Ram Bharosa. 'That's only for memsahibs. Where did you get it?'

'Someone gave it to me—for my necklace.'

'You exchanged it for your lucky claw!'

Binya nodded. 'But what do you need it for? The sun isn't hot enough, and it isn't meant for the rain. It's just a pretty thing for rich ladies to play with!'

Binya nodded and smiled again. Ram Bharosa was quite right; it was just a beautiful plaything. And that was exactly why she had fallen in love with it.

'I have an idea,' said the shopkeeper. 'It's no use to you, that umbrella. Why not sell it to me? I'll give you five rupees for it.'

'It's worth fifteen,' said Binya.

'Well, then, I'll give you ten.'

Binya laughed and shook her head.

'Twelve rupees?' said Ram Bharosa, but without much hope.

Binya placed a five-paise coin on the counter.

'I came for a toffee,' she said.

Ram Bharosa pulled at his drooping

whiskers, gave Binya a wry look, and placed a toffee in the palm of her hand. He watched Binya as she walked away along the dusty road. The blue umbrella held him fascinated, and he stared after it until it was out of sight.

The villagers used this road to go to the market town. Some used the bus, a few rode on mules, and most people walked. Today, everyone on the road turned their heads to stare at the girl with the bright blue umbrella.

Binya sat down in the shade of a pine tree. The umbrella, still open, lay beside her. She cradled her head in her arms, and presently she dozed off. It was that kind of day, sleepily warm and summery.

And while she slept, a wind sprang up.

It came quietly, swishing gently through the trees, humming softly. Then it was joined by other random gusts, bustling over the tops of the mountains. The trees shook their heads and came to life. The wind fanned Binya's cheeks.

The umbrella stirred on the grass.

The wind grew stronger, picking up dead leaves and sending them spinning and swirling through the air. It got into the umbrella and began to drag it over the grass. Suddenly it lifted the umbrella and carried it about six feet from the sleeping girl. The sound woke Binya.

She was on her feet immediately, and then she was leaping down the steep slope. But just as she was within reach of the umbrella, the wind picked it up again and carried it further downhill.

Binya set off in pursuit. The wind was in a wicked, playful mood. It would leave the umbrella alone for a few moments but as soon as Binya came near, it would pick up the umbrella again and send it bouncing, floating, dancing away from her.

The hill grew steeper. Binya knew that after twenty yards it would fall away in a precipice. She ran faster. And the wind ran with her, ahead of her, and the blue umbrella stayed up with the wind.

A fresh gust picked it up and carried it to the very edge of the cliff. There it balanced for a few seconds, before toppling over, out of sight.

Binya ran to the edge of the cliff. Going down on her hands and knees, she peered down the cliff face. About a hundred feet below, a small stream rushed between great boulders. Hardly anything grew on the cliff face—just a few stunted bushes, and, halfway down, a wild cherry tree growing crookedly out of the rocks and hanging across the chasm. The umbrella had stuck in the cherry tree.

Binya didn't hesitate. She may have been timid with strangers, but she was at home on a hillside. She stuck her bare leg over the edge of the cliff and began climbing down. She kept her face to the hillside, feeling her way with her feet, only changing her handhold when she knew her feet were secure. Sometimes she held on to the thorny bilberry bushes, but she did not trust the other plants, which came away very easily.

Loose stones rattled down the cliff. Once on their way, the stones did not stop until they reached the bottom of the hill; and they took other stones with them, so that there was soon a cascade of stones, and Binya had to be very careful not to start a landslide.

As agile as a mountain goat, she did not take more than five minutes to reach the crooked cherry tree. But the most difficult task remained—she had to crawl along the trunk of the tree, which stood out at right angles from the cliff. Only by doing this could she reach the trapped umbrella.

Binya felt no fear when climbing trees. She was proud of the fact that she could climb them as well as Bijju. Gripping the rough cherry bark with her toes, and using her knees as leverage, she crawled along the trunk of the projecting tree until she was almost within reach of the umbrella. She noticed with dismay that the blue cloth was torn in a couple of places.

She looked down, and it was only then that she felt afraid. She was right over the chasm, balanced precariously about eighty feet above the boulder-strewn stream. Looking down, she felt quite dizzy. Her hands shook, and the tree shook too. If she slipped now, there was only one direction in which she could fall—down, down, into the depths of that dark and shadowy ravine.

There was only one thing to do; concentrate on the patch of blue just a couple of feet away from her. She did not look down or up, but straight ahead, and willing herself forward, she managed to reach the umbrella.

She could not crawl back with it in her hands. So, after dislodging it from the forked branch in which it had stuck, she let it fall, still open, into the ravine below.

Cushioned by the wind, the umbrella floated serenely downwards, landing in a thicket of nettles.

Binya crawled back along the trunk of the cherry tree. Twenty minutes later, she emerged from the nettle clump, her precious umbrella held aloft. She had nettle stings all over her legs, but she was hardly aware of the smarting. She was as immune to nettles as Bijju was to bees.

III

About four years previously, Bijju had knocked a hive out of an oak tree, and had been badly stung on the face and legs. It had been a painful experience. But now, if a bee stung him, he felt nothing at all: he had been immunized for life!

He was on his way home from school. It was two o'clock and he hadn't eaten since six in the morning. Fortunately, the kingora bushes—the bilberries—were in fruit, and already Bijju's lips were stained purple with the juice of the wild, sour fruit.

He didn't have any money to spend at Ram Bharosa's shop, but he stopped there anyway to look at the sweets in their glass jars.

'And what will you have today?' asked Ram Bharosa.

'No money,' said Bijju.

'You can pay me later.'

Bijju shook his head. Some of his friends had taken sweets on credit, and at the end of the month they had found they'd eaten more sweets than they could possibly pay for! As a result, they'd had to hand over to Ram Bharosa some of their most treasured possessions—such as a curved knife for cutting grass, or a small hand-axe, or a jar for pickles, or a pair of earrings—and these had become the shopkeeper's possessions and were kept by him or sold in his shop.

Ram Bharosa had set his heart on having Binya's blue umbrella, and so naturally he was anxious to give credit to either of the children, but so far neither had fallen into the trap.

Bijju moved on, his mouth full of kingora berries. Halfway home, he saw Binya with the cows. It was late evening, and the sun had gone down, but Binya still had the umbrella open. The two small rents had been stitched up by her mother.

Bijju gave his sister a handful of berries. She handed him the umbrella while she ate the berries.

'You can have the umbrella until we get home,' she said. It was her way of rewarding Bijju for bringing her the wild fruit.

Calling 'Neelu! Gori!' Binya and Bijju set out for home, followed at some distance by the cows.

It was dark before they reached the village, but Bijju still had the umbrella open.

Most of the people in the village were a little envious of Binya's blue umbrella. No one else had ever possessed one like it. The schoolmaster's wife thought it was quite wrong for a poor cultivator's daughter to have such a fine umbrella while she, a second-class BA, had to make do with an ordinary black one. Her husband offered to have their old umbrella dyed blue; she gave him a scornful look, and loved him a little less than before. The pujari, who looked after the temple, announced that he would buy a multicoloured umbrella the next time he was in the town. A few days later he returned looking annoyed and grumbling that they weren't available except in Delhi. Most people consoled themselves by saying that Binya's pretty umbrella wouldn't keep out the rain, if it rained heavily; that it would shrivel in the sun, if the sun was fierce; that it would collapse in a wind, if the wind was strong; that it would attract lightning, if lightning fell near it; and that it would prove unlucky, if there was any ill luck going about. Secretly, everyone admired it.

Unlike the adults, the children didn't have to pretend. They were full of praise for the umbrella. It was so light, so pretty, so bright a blue! And it was just the right size for Binya. They knew that if they said nice things about the umbrella, Binya would smile and give it to them to hold for a little while—just a very little while!

Soon, it was the time of the monsoon. Big black clouds kept piling up, and thunder rolled over the hills.

Binya sat on the hillside all afternoon, waiting for the rain. As soon as the first big drop of rain came down, she raised the umbrella over her head. More drops, big ones, came pattering down. She could see them through the umbrella silk, as they broke against the cloth.

And then there was a cloudburst, and it was like standing under a waterfall. The umbrella wasn't really a rain umbrella, but it held up bravely. Only Binya's feet got wet. Rods of rain fell around her in a curtain of shivered glass.

Everywhere on the hillside people were scurrying for shelter. Some made for a charcoal burner's hut, others for a mule-shed, or Ram Bharosa's shop. Binya was the only one who didn't run. This was what she'd been waiting for—rain on her umbrella—and she wasn't in a hurry to go home. She didn't mind getting her feet wet. The cows didn't mind getting wet either.

Presently she found Bijju sheltering in a cave. He would have enjoyed getting wet, but he had his schoolbooks with him and he couldn't afford to let them get spoilt. When he saw Binya, he came out of the cave and shared the umbrella. He was a head taller than his sister, so he had to hold the umbrella for her, while she held his books.

The cows had been left far behind.

'Neelu, Neelu!' called Binya. 'Gori!' called Bijju. When their mother saw them sauntering home through the driving rain, she called out: 'Binya! Bijju! Hurry up, and bring the cows in! What are you doing out there in the rain?'

'Just testing the umbrella,' said Bijju.

IV

The rains set in, and the sun only made brief appearances.

The hills turned a lush green. Ferns sprang up on walls and tree trunks. Giant lilies reared up like leopards from the tall grass. A white mist coiled and uncoiled as it floated up from the valley. It was a beautiful season, except for the leeches.

Every day, Binya came home with a couple of leeches fastened to the flesh of her bare legs. They fell off by themselves just as soon as they'd had their thimbleful of blood, but you didn't know they were on you until they fell off, and then, later, the skin became very sore and itchy. Some of the older people still believed that to be bled by leeches was a remedy for various ailments. Whenever Ram Bharosa had a headache, he applied a leech to his throbbing temple.

Three days of incessant rain had flooded out a number of small animals who lived in holes in the ground. Binya's mother suddenly found the roof full of field rats. She had to drive them out; they ate too much of her stored-up wheat flour and rice. Bijju liked lifting up large rocks to disturb the scorpions who were sleeping beneath. And snakes came out to bask in the sun.

Binya had just crossed the small stream at the bottom of the hill when she saw something gliding out of the bushes and coming towards her. It was a long black snake. A clatter of loose stones frightened it. Seeing the girl in its way, it rose up, hissing, prepared to strike. The forked tongue darted out, the venomous head lunged at Binya.

Binya's umbrella was open as usual. She thrust it forward, between herself and the snake, and the snake's hard snout thudded twice against the strong silk of the umbrella. The reptile then turned and slithered away over the wet rocks, disappearing into a clump of ferns.

Binya forgot about the cows and ran all the way home to tell her mother how she had been saved by the umbrella. Bijju had to put away his books and go out to fetch the cows. He carried a stout stick, in case he met with any snakes.

First, the summer sun, and now the endless rain, meant that the umbrella was beginning to fade a little. From a bright blue it had changed to a light blue. But it was still a pretty thing, and tougher than it looked, and Ram Bharosa still desired it. He did not want to sell it; he wanted to own it. He was probably the richest man in the area—so why shouldn't he have a blue umbrella? Not a day passed without his getting a glimpse of Binya and the umbrella; and the more he saw the umbrella, the more he wanted it.

The schools closed during the monsoon, but this didn't mean that Bijju could sit at home doing nothing. Neelu and Gori were providing more milk than was required at home, so Binya's mother was able to sell a kilo of milk every day: half a kilo to the schoolmaster, and half a kilo (at a reduced rate) to the temple pujari. Bijju had to deliver the milk every morning.

Ram Bharosa had asked Bijju to work in his shop during the holidays, but Bijju didn't have time—he had to help his mother with the ploughing and the transplanting of the rice seedlings. So, Ram Bharosa employed a boy from the next village, a boy called Rajaram. He did all the washing-up, and ran various errands. He went to the same school as Bijju, but the two boys were not friends.

One day, as Binya passed the shop, twirling her blue umbrella, Rajaram noticed that his employer gave a deep sigh and began muttering to himself.

'What's the matter, Babuji?' asked the boy.

'Oh, nothing,' said Ram Bharosa. 'It's just a sickness that has come upon me. And it's all due to that girl Binya and her wretched umbrella.'

'Why, what has she done to you?'

'Refused to sell me her umbrella! There's pride for you. And I offered her ten rupees.'

'Perhaps, if you gave her twelve....'

'But it isn't new any longer. It isn't worth eight rupees now. All the same, I'd like to have it.'

'You wouldn't make a profit on it,' said Rajaram.

'It's not the profit I'm after, wretch! It's the thing itself. It's the beauty of it!'

'And what would you do with it, Babuji? You don't visit anyone—you're seldom out of your shop. Of what use would it be to you?'

'Of what use is a poppy in a cornfield? Of what use is a rainbow? Of what use are you, numbskull? Wretch! I, too, have a soul. I want the umbrella, because—because I want its beauty to be mine!'

Rajaram put the kettle on to boil, began dusting the counter, all the time muttering: 'I'm as useful as an umbrella,' and then, after a short period of intense thought, said: 'What will you give me, Babuji, if I get the umbrella for you?'

'What do you mean?' asked the old man.

'You know what I mean. What will you give me?'

'You mean to steal it, don't you, you wretch? What a delightful child you are! I'm glad you're not my son or my enemy. But look, everyone will know it has been stolen, and then how will I be able to show off with it?'

'You will have to gaze upon it in secret,' said Rajaram with a chuckle. 'Or take it into Tehri, and have it coloured red! That's your problem. But tell me, Babuji, do you want it badly enough to pay me three rupees for stealing it without being seen?'

Ram Bharosa gave the boy a long, sad look. 'You're a sharp boy,' he said. 'You'll come to a bad end. I'll give you two rupees.'

'Three,' said the boy.

'Two,' said the old man.

'You don't really want it, I can see that,' said the boy.

'Wretch!' said the old man. 'Evil one!

Darkener of my doorstep! Fetch me the umbrella, and I'll give you three rupees.'

V

Binya was in the forest glade where she had first seen the umbrella. No one came there for picnics during the monsoon. The grass was always wet and the pine needles were slippery underfoot. The tall trees shut out the light, and poisonous-looking mushrooms, orange and purple, sprang up everywhere. But it was a good place for porcupines, who seemed to like the mushrooms, and Binya was searching for porcupine quills.

The hill people didn't think much of porcupine quills, but far away in southern India, the quills were valued as charms and sold at a rupee each. So, Ram Bharosa paid a tenth of a rupee for each quill brought to him, and he in turn sold the quills at a profit to a trader from the plains.

Binya had already found five quills, and she knew there'd be more in the long grass. For once, she'd put her umbrella down. She had to put it aside if she was to search the ground thoroughly.

It was Rajaram's chance.

He'd been following Binya for some time, concealing himself behind trees and rocks, creeping closer whenever she became absorbed in her search. He was anxious that she should not see him and be able to recognize him later.

He waited until Binya had wandered some distance from the umbrella. Then, running forward at a crouch, he seized the open umbrella and dashed off with it.

But Rajaram had very big feet. Binya heard his heavy footsteps and turned just in time to see him as he disappeared between the trees. She cried out, dropped the porcupine quills, and gave chase.

Binya was swift and sure-footed, but Rajaram

had a long stride. All the same, he made the mistake of running downhill. A long-legged person is much faster going uphill than down. Binya reached the edge of the forest glade in time to see the thief scrambling down the path to the stream. He had closed the umbrella so that it would not hinder his flight.

Binya was beginning to gain on the boy. He kept to the path, while she simply slid and leapt down the steep hillside. Near the bottom of the hill the path began to straighten out, and it was here that the long-legged boy began to forge ahead again.

Bijju was coming home from another direction. He had a bundle of sticks which he'd collected for the kitchen fire. As he reached the path, he saw Binya rushing down the hill as though all the mountain spirits in Garhwal were after her.

'What's wrong?' he called. 'Why are you running?'

Binya paused only to point at the fleeing Rajaram.

'My umbrella!' she cried. 'He has stolen it!'

Bijju dropped his bundle of sticks, and ran after his sister. When he reached her side, he said, 'I'll soon catch him!' and went sprinting away over the lush green grass. He was fresh, and he was soon well ahead of Binya and gaining on the thief.

Rajaram was crossing the shallow stream when Bijju caught up with him. Rajaram was the taller boy, but Bijju was much stronger. He flung himself at the thief, caught him by the legs, and brought him down in the water. Rajaram got to his feet and tried to drag himself away, but Bijju still had him by a leg. Rajaram overbalanced and came down with a great splash. He had to let the umbrella fall. It began to float away on the current. Just then Binya arrived, flushed and breathless, and went dashing into the stream after the umbrella.

Meanwhile, a tremendous fight was taking place. Locked in fierce combat, the two boys swayed together on a rock, tumbled on to the sand, rolled over and over the pebbled bank until they were again thrashing about in the shallows of the stream. The magpies, bulbuls, and other birds were disturbed, and flew away with cries of alarm.

Covered with mud, gasping and spluttering, the boys groped for each other in the water. After five minutes of frenzied struggle, Bijju emerged victorious.

Rajaram lay flat on his back on the sand, exhausted, while Bijju sat astride him, pinning him down with his arms and legs.

'Let me get up!' gasped Rajaram. 'Let me go—I don't want your useless umbrella!'

'Then why did you take it?' demanded Bijju. 'Come on—tell me why!'

'It was that skinflint Ram Bharosa,' said Rajaram. 'He told me to get it for him. He said if I didn't fetch it, I'd lose my job.'

By early October, the rains were coming to an end. The leeches disappeared. The ferns turned yellow, and the sunlight on the green hills was mellow and golden, like the limes on the small tree in front of Binya's home. Bijju's days were happy ones as he came home from school, munching on roasted corn. Binya's umbrella had turned a pale milky blue, and was patched in several places, but it was still the prettiest umbrella in the village, and she still carried it with her wherever she went.

The cold, cruel winter wasn't far off, but somehow October seems longer than other months, because it is a kind month: the grass is good to be upon, the breeze is warm and gentle and pine-scented. That October, everyone seemed contented—everyone, that is, except Ram Bharosa.

The old man had by now given up all hope of ever possessing Binya's umbrella. He wished he had never set eyes on it. Because of the umbrella, he had suffered the tortures of greed, the despair of loneliness. Because of the umbrella, people had stopped coming to his shop!

Ever since it had become known that Ram Bharosa had tried to have the umbrella stolen, the village people had turned against him. They stopped trusting the old man; instead of buying their soap and tea and matches from his shop, they preferred to walk an extra mile to the shops near the Tehri bus stand. Who would have dealings with a man who had sold his soul for an umbrella? The children taunted him, twisted his name around. From 'Ram the Trustworthy' he became 'Trusty Umbrella Thief'.

The old man sat alone in his empty shop, listening to the eternal hissing of his kettle and wondering if anyone would ever again step in for a glass of tea. Ram Bharosa had lost his own appetite, and ate and drank very little. There was no money coming in. He had his savings in a bank in Tehri, but it was a terrible thing to have to dip into them! To save money, he had dismissed the blundering Rajaram. So, he was left without any company. The roof leaked and the wind got in through the corrugated tin sheets, but Ram Bharosa didn't care.

Bijju and Binya passed his shop almost every day. Bijju went by with a loud but tuneless whistle. He was one of the world's whistlers; cares rested lightly on his shoulders. But, strangely enough, Binya crept quietly past the shop, looking the other way, almost as though she was in some way responsible for the misery of Ram Bharosa.

She kept reasoning with herself, telling herself that the umbrella was her very own, and that she couldn't help it if others were jealous of it. But had she loved the umbrella too much? Had it mattered more to her than people mattered? She couldn't help feeling that, in a small way, she was the cause of the sad look on Ram Bharosa's face ('His face is a yard long,' said Bijju) and the ruinous condition of his shop. It was all due to his own greed, no doubt, but she didn't want him to feel too bad about what he'd done, because it made her feel bad about herself; and so, she closed the umbrella whenever she came near the shop, opening it again only when she was out of sight.

One day, towards the end of October, when she had ten paise in her pocket, she entered the shop and asked the old man for a toffee.

She was Ram Bharosa's first customer in almost two weeks. He looked suspiciously at the girl. Had she come to taunt him, to flaunt the umbrella in his face? She had placed her coin on the counter. Perhaps it was a bad coin. Ram Bharosa picked it up and bit it; he held it up to the light; he rang it on the ground. It was a good coin. He gave Binya the toffee.

Binya had already left the shop when Ram Bharosa saw the closed umbrella lying on his counter. There it was, the blue umbrella he had always wanted, within his grasp at last! He had only to hide it at the back of his shop, and no one would know that he had it, no one could prove that Binya had left it behind.

He stretched out his trembling, bony hand, and took the umbrella by the handle. He pressed it open. He stood beneath it, in the dark shadows of his shop, where no sun or rain could ever touch it.

'But I'm never in the sun or in the rain,' he said aloud. 'Of what use is an umbrella to me?'

And he hurried outside and ran after Binya.

'Binya, Binya!' he shouted. 'Binya, you've

left your umbrella behind!'

He wasn't used to running, but he caught up with her, held out the umbrella, saying, 'You forgot it—the umbrella!'

In that moment it belonged to both of them.

But Binya didn't take the umbrella. She shook her head and said, 'You keep it. I don't need it any more.'

'But it's such a pretty umbrella!' protested Ram Bharosa. 'It's the best umbrella in the village.'

'I know,' said Binya. 'But an umbrella isn't everything.'

And she left the old man holding the umbrella, and went tripping down the road, and there was nothing between her and the bright blue sky.

VI

Well, now that Ram Bharosa has the blue umbrella—a gift from Binya, as he tells everyone—he is sometimes persuaded to go out into the sun or the rain, and as a result he looks much healthier. Sometimes he uses the umbrella to chase away pigs or goats. It is always left open outside the shop, and anyone who wants to borrow it may do so; and so, in a way it has become everyone's umbrella. It is faded and patchy, but it is still the best umbrella in the village.

People are visiting Ram Bharosa's shop again. Whenever Bijju or Binya stop for a cup of tea, he gives them a little extra milk or sugar. They like their tea sweet and milky.

A few nights ago, a bear visited Ram Bharosa's shop. There had been snow on the higher ranges of the Himalaya, and the bear had been finding it difficult to obtain food; so, it had come lower down, to see what it could pick up near the village. That night it scrambled on to the tin roof of Ram Bharosa's shop, and made off with a huge pumpkin which had been ripening on the roof. But in climbing off the roof, the bear had lost a claw.

Next morning Ram Bharosa found the claw just outside the door of his shop. He picked it up and put it in his pocket. A bear's claw was a lucky find.

A day later, when he went into the market town, he took the claw with him, and left it with a silversmith, giving the craftsman certain instructions. The silversmith made a locket for the claw, then he gave it a thin silver chain. When Ram Bharosa came again, he paid the silversmith ten rupees for his work.

The days were growing shorter, and Binya had to be home a little earlier every evening. There was a hungry leopard at large, and she couldn't leave the cows out after dark.

She was hurrying past Ram Bharosa's shop when the old man called out to her.

'Binya, spare a minute! I want to show you something.'

Binya stepped into the shop.

'What do you think of it?' asked Ram Bharosa, showing her the silver pendant with the claw.

'It's so beautiful,' said Binya, just touching the claw and the silver chain.

'It's a bear's claw,' said Ram Bharosa. 'That's even luckier than a leopard's claw. Would you like to have it?'

'I have no money,' said Binya.

'That doesn't matter. You gave me the umbrella, I give you the claw! Come, let's see what it looks like on you.'

He placed the pendant on Binya, and indeed it looked very beautiful on her.

Ram Bharosa says he will never forget the smile she gave him when she left the shop.

She was halfway home when she realized she had left the cows behind.

'Neelu, Neelu!' she called. 'Oh, Gori!'

There was a faint tinkle of bells as the cows

came slowly down the mountain path.

In the distance she could hear her mother and Bijju calling for her.

She began to sing. They heard her singing, and knew she was safe and near.

She walked home through the darkening glade, singing of the stars, and the trees stood still and listened to her, and the mountains were glad.

VIKRAM AND THE BETAAL: A RETELLING
STEPHEN ALTER

The original version of this story cycle was composed in the eleventh century by a poet from Kashmir, Somdev Bhatt, and titled *Betaal Pachisi*, or 'The Twenty-five Stories of the Betaal'. In 1870, it was translated into English by Richard Burton and retitled *Vikram and the Vampire*. In recent years, other renditions have emerged, as well as film and television adaptations. This retelling attempts to condense and distil the story for younger readers.

King Vikramaditya was a wise and courageous ruler. Wealthy yet generous, powerful but compassionate, he was both a warrior as well as a lover of art and poetry. His capital, the ancient city of Ujjain, lay on the banks of the river Shipra. Many people, from all over India and the rest of the world, visited his court where he welcomed them equally and without exception. One day, a merchant arrived at the palace and presented the king with an unusual piece of fruit. It was neither a peach nor a pear, not a melon or an apple, but something entirely new and exotic. The king thanked the merchant for his gift, which was put away safely in a storeroom in the palace.

The following day, the merchant appeared once again and presented the king with another identical piece of fruit. This continued for many days until the storeroom was full. Finally, the king decided to taste this strange and wonderful delicacy. But as soon as the fruit was cut open, instead of a seed at its centre, Vikram discovered a ruby as large as an apricot stone. Immediately, the king ordered all of the fruit in the storeroom to be inspected and his courtiers confirmed that each and every one contained a ruby.

Astonished by these lavish gifts, Vikram asked the merchant what he might offer in return, promising to grant him anything he wished. After protesting politely that he sought no favours and showering the king with as many compliments as there were rubies, the merchant was finally persuaded to suggest some compensation for the tribute he had offered. Bowing before the king, the merchant requested that Vikram meet him in the evening, under a banyan tree on the banks of the river Shipra, outside the city walls of Ujjain, near the cremation grounds where final rites were conducted for the dead.

The king and his courtiers were puzzled and alarmed. The prime minister and other royal advisers counselled Vikram to not accede to the merchant's request, but the king was adamant that he would fulfil his promise. He agreed to meet the merchant after sunset, accompanied only by his son and heir, Prince Vikramasena.

Leaving the gates of Ujjain, as darkness fell, the two brave warriors set off alone for the banyan tree. All around them funeral pyres were burning and in the dancing light of the dying flames they saw ghosts and ghouls, demons and evil spirits, fierce-looking phantoms and ferocious beasts. With their swords drawn, the king and the prince advanced towards the tree, which had many limbs and twisted vines, extending in all directions like a forest in and of itself. Beneath the gloomy shadows of the banyan, they saw the merchant sitting cross-legged on the ground. He was wearing a cotton loincloth and his skin was smeared with ash, while his long hair fell below his shoulders. No longer the courteous trader who had graced the court, the merchant had transformed himself into a sadhu who practised severe austerities and possessed magical powers.

'Who are you?' Vikram demanded, prepared to cut off the man's head with his sword if he threatened them.

'A wandering mendicant who lives off the charity of others,' the sadhu replied, holding up a begging bowl fashioned from a human skull.

'What is it you want of us?' the king inquired, his voice loud and confident.

The sadhu cringed, though his eyes glowed like embers.

'A simple favour,' he said. 'Nothing that bold warriors like you cannot accomplish.'

Prince Vikramasena trembled as he stood beside his father, while a host of spirits and spectres looked down upon them from the shadowy branches of the tree.

'Out with it!' the king shouted. 'Tell us what you want.'

'Over there, beyond the edge of the cremation grounds, stands a siras tree,' said the sadhu, pointing upriver, where the darkness was as black as a calligrapher's inkwell. 'It is covered with blossoms, as fragrant and delicate as any flowers can be. In the leafy branches of that tree lives a betaal, the ghost of a man who died some years ago. Nobody performed his funeral rites, so he lingers on, suspended between life and death. My only request, noble king, is that you catch the betaal and bring him to me.'

'What purpose will that serve?' the king inquired, perplexed.

'No purpose at all, beyond the dictates of fate,' said the sadhu, reaching into a hollow within the roots of the banyan tree and producing a frayed and tattered sack, which he handed to the king.

'What am I to do with this?' Vikramaditya said with disgust, for the sack was filthy and smelled of rotting fish.

'Use this to capture the betaal and carry him

back here,' the sadhu replied. 'It is a magical sack, woven out of snakeskins shed by cobras that live in this tree and the fibres of potent wild herbs and stinging nettles. Beware, for the betaal is a clever and treacherous ghost. He will trick you with his stories and mesmerize you with his words.'

Determined to fulfil his promise and return to the comforts of his palace as swiftly as possible, Vikram gestured for his son to follow as they set off to find the siras tree. Cautiously, but without hesitation, they made their way through the charred and smouldering remains of funeral pyres, the air thick with the stench of smoke. All around them they could hear the howling and wailing of terrifying spirits and grotesque creatures that haunted the riverbank. Eventually, they came to the siras tree. Its blossoms emitted an ethereal glow and their fragrance filled the air, a perfume that erased the pall of death.

Glancing up into the branches overhead, Vikram searched for the betaal but there seemed to be no sign of the spirit. Then, as his eyes adjusted to the faint luminescence of the flowers, he saw what looked like a cobweb suspended between the highest limbs. Nothing more than a gauze-like shadow, it seemed to have been woven out of colourless threads, hanging lifeless as a shroud in the tree. While the prince stood guard below, Vikram climbed into the siras and cut the web free with his sword.

Immediately, a frantic rustling sound filled the air, like a flock of birds taking flight, or a sudden gust of wind shaking dead leaves. Vikram felt the filaments of the cobweb whirling about him in the darkness. But full of resolve and undeterred by the chaos that engulfed him, the king opened the sack and swiftly caught the invisible betaal, like a fish in a net. Closing the mouth of the sack, he held it tightly with a firm grip as the captive spirit wriggled and squirmed, trying to escape.

Climbing down from the tree, the king slung the sack over one shoulder and told the prince to follow close behind, with his sword unsheathed. Moments later, as they set off, both men heard a voice.

'Hail to thee, King Vikramaditya of Ujjain!' the betaal said in a cynical, mocking tone. 'You govern your subjects with absolute power, but here you are nothing. You may rule over the living but not the dead. When I was alive, I bowed before you and praised your name but now I am free!'

The betaal had a voice like a dry wind sighing through brittle grass, a hoarse whisper that murmured in the king's ear.

'Silence!' Vikram cried. 'You faceless fiend!'

But the spirit just laughed, prodding the king's back with a painful kick.

'Go on! Get going! Hurry up!' said the

betaal. 'Do as you were told by the sadhu who sits beneath the banyan tree. Tonight, you are no longer a king, but a beast of burden carrying me on your back, like a humble donkey doing his master's bidding. Move along, Vikram… while I tell you a story to pass the time….'

'Insolent swine!' the king cursed. 'I will kill you if you don't hold your tongue!'

'Ha ha!' said betaal with a sarcastic chuckle, 'You can't harm me. I am dead already. Now listen to this…and be silent, or else I will squirm my way out of this wretched sack and fly back to my tree.'

Desperate to rid himself of the invisible spirit, Vikram hurried on towards the distant banyan tree, which was silhouetted against the glimmering flames of the burning ghats. As they proceeded, the betaal recounted a romantic tale about a prince named Vajramakut, who went hunting in the forest where he came upon a beautiful maiden, Padmavati. The two of them fell instantly in love and were soon married. This sentimental story annoyed the king, who preferred to hear accounts of bravery and valour, though it intrigued his son, who became engrossed in the fanciful romance. But heeding the betaal's warning, neither of them spoke or interrupted the tale, for fear of driving the spirit away. Before they reached the sadhu's tree, however, the ghostly raconteur concluded his story with an ironic tragedy of errors in which the prince and his bride were tricked into deceiving each other and fell out of love.

'Now, here is the riddle!' the betaal announced, with a malevolent hiss. 'Think carefully, Vikram, before you answer my question. In this sad farce of love, neither party was innocent but, tell me, who bore the greater blame? Was it the prince, Vajra? Or the princess, Padma?'

'Of course I know the answer,' Vikram snapped, unable to remain silent any longer. As king, he was used to making pronouncements and always having the last word. 'In matters of love, it is the woman who always deceives the man!'

By this time, they had passed beneath the outermost branches of the spreading banyan and the sadhu's eyes were upon them, watching greedily as the king approached to deliver his awful burden. But, in a flash, he felt the betaal squeeze through the mouth of the sack and with hysterical screams of laughter, it flew away into the night.

'Wrong! Wrong answer!' the ghost shouted and from all around the riverbank, the other spirits and demons cried out in taunting chorus. 'Wrong! Wrong! Wrong!'

Disheartened but intent upon their task, King Vikram and the prince retraced their steps to the siras tree. Once again, they found the betaal's shroud suspended like a spider's web between two high branches. Ascending the tree, Vikram cut the web loose, exactly as he'd done the first time, and trapped the malicious spirit in the odorous but magical sack. Then, just as before, the betaal spoke in a snide and scurrilous voice, warning the king to remain silent as he began to narrate another tale. A while later, as they approached their destination, the storyteller provoked the king with a question, to which Vikram blurted out an impulsive reply that sent the betaal flying back to his perch. This happened again and again. Most of the betaal's stories were beguiling tales of human frailty and folly. But one of these intrigued the prince more than all of the others.

'Here's another parable for you, Your Highness...' the narrator began, 'yet another enchanting episode of love and innocence. Remember, you must listen to my words without interrupting, or I will slough off this stinking sack and return directly to my tree.'

'Get on with it, then!' Vikram muttered under his breath. 'But keep it short and to the point!'

With a snort of laughter, the betaal continued: 'Long ago, there was a time when men could understand the speech of birds and those winged creatures of the sky had taught themselves the language of man. In a kingdom far away lived a prince named Raja Ram, who had a pet parakeet called Churaman. They would speak to each other constantly, chattering on like close companions and confidants. One day the prince inquired of the parakeet, 'Tell me, my feathered friend, whom shall I marry?' The parakeet quickly answered, 'In the land of Magadh lives a princess named Chandravati. She is the perfect match for you.'

'Now, it so happened that Chandravati also had a pet bird, a mynah named Manjari, with whom she shared her closest secrets and prattled on about those matters that women discuss amongst themselves. Eventually, the subject of marriage came up, and Chandravati asked her mynah for advice. The bird promptly replied, proposing Raja Ram's name. 'He is handsome and brave,' the mynah opined. 'One day he will surely be king and you, his queen.' Envoys were dispatched from the two kingdoms and the marriage was negotiated and settled in short order, much to the delight of the prince and princess. Soon after their wedding was celebrated and blessed, the happy couple decided that since the two birds had brought them together, Churaman and Manjari should also be married. Immediately, the princess put the parakeet and the mynah together in the same cage and priests were called to perform the avian nuptials. But even before the last flower petals had been sprinkled on the cage and the shehnai had ceased its joyous music, the two birds began to squabble. Soon, their quarrel became so violent that the prince was forced to open the cage, and the parakeet and mynah flew out. Escaping through an open window, they never came back.'

The betaal paused for a moment, seeing that they were now within earshot of the sadhu, who sat impatiently under the banyan's branches, awaiting their arrival.

'So, here's my question, good King Vikram,' exclaimed the betaal.

The prince caught his father's eye, warning him with a subtle gesture not to fall prey to the ghost's mischief.

'Who was more foolish, the princess who placed the two birds in the same cage, or the prince who set them both free?' the betaal whispered from within the foetid confines of the sack. Resisting an urge to answer, the king kept his lips sealed, though the spirit prompted him petulantly, 'Quickly now. What's the correct answer?'

After a brief silence, when Vikram was about

to deposit his burden in front of the sadhu, the betaal cried out. 'Ha! If you won't answer that question, here's another! Who do you think is cleverer, a man who learns the speech of birds, or a bird that learns to speak like men?'

'The man, of course!' Vikram exclaimed, before he could stop himself. 'The birds are only imitating the sounds we make while a man who translates birdsong is much wiser than them!'

'Wrong again!' the betaal screeched with glee as he broke loose from the sack and vanished into the moonless night, urged on by a hideous throng of chanting spirits.

Though weary and discouraged by their repeated failures, King Vikram and the prince returned to the siris tree and captured the betaal one more time. He kicked and struggled inside the sack when Vikram slung it over his shoulder. By now, the night had almost ended and the dark sky had begun to brighten along the edges, a faint light seeping over the horizon.

When the insidious narrator began a new tale, Vikram warned him to be silent.

'No more stories!' the king bellowed. 'I've had enough of your nonsense.'

The betaal lay still for a moment, as if chastened by Vikram's warning but as they started on their way again, his voice emerged once more, though he spoke in a quieter, more respectful tone, without his chiding insolence.

'There is but one story left,' he said. 'It is the most important tale of all....'

'I said, NO MORE!' Vikram warned him.

'But this is your story, O King, and it must be told before the sun rises over Ujjain,' the betaal pleaded. 'You must hear me out, if you want to know your fate.'

The king and the prince exchanged wary glances, not sure if they should trust this voluble phantom who had tricked them so many times already. But as he began to speak, they found themselves listening to the story of the merchant who had visited their court and presented Vikram with the strange and wondrous fruit. The betaal knew every detail of those events and described precisely how the rubies were discovered and the obsequious manner by which the merchant had ingratiated himself with the king. He also recounted how a promise was extracted from the king that he would visit the cremation grounds after sunset the night before.

'How do you know all this?' Vikram cried out with alarm.

'Because my fate is tied to yours,' the betaal answered. 'This man is not a merchant but a tantric sorcerer, who came to your court with nefarious designs. He preys on both the living and the dead, gaining his evil powers from the ash of funeral pyres and the spirits that haunt this place. You have seen him, sitting beneath the banyan tree, pretending to be a simple ascetic but he is more dangerous than any of the ghouls and demons that inhabit the shores of the river Shipra. Beware, King Vikram, for he plans to enslave me in his wicked scheme. By exploiting my miserable fate, he will destroy yours. With his poisonous spells and corrupt magic, he plans to use me to kill you and the prince, so that he can take over your kingdom and destroy Ujjain.'

'Why should I believe you?' Vikram demanded, seeing that daybreak was almost upon them, and the dark shape of the banyan stood out against a brightening sky, as did the rooftops and domes of the city.

'This time, I will not run away,' the betaal announced, 'and when you deliver me to him, you will see how he seizes this infernal sack, as if it were filled with gold. Then you can make your choice, wise king, and answer the simple dilemma. Have I lied? Or have I told you the truth? It is a question upon which your life depends.'

By now, they had arrived in front of the sadhu. Pausing, Vikram studied the gaunt ascetic sitting cross-legged on the ground, his skin daubed with ash and his hair hanging in dreadlocks. The begging bowl made from a skull was balanced on his knee.

Lowering the sack from his shoulder, Vikram flung it on the ground in front of the sadhu, just as the sun began to appear in the east. With a triumphant gasp, the tantric lunged forward and gripped the mouth of the sack with both hands to prevent the betaal from escaping. But as he did this, Vikram drew his sword and cut off the sadhu's head in a single stroke.

After their long ordeal, Vikram and his son returned to the palace where they were greeted with relief and celebration by the assembled courtiers, who had been anxiously awaiting their arrival all night. As sunlight shone on the river, the king reassured his loyal subjects that all was well and danger had been averted. Then summoning his royal priests, he ordered them to perform final rites for the betaal to release him from his unfortunate state, allowing him to pass from this life into the next.

THE BOUTIQUE

SHASHI THAROOR

The liftman swung open the door of the elevator and looked at Amma and me with an appraisingly critical eye.

From his manner it was clear he wasn't very impressed; Amma in her plain cotton sari with her slightly greying hair done up in a traditional way at the back, clutching the invitation card as if for security and looking very plain and rather proletarian; me in my loose kurta that fell awkwardly from bony shoulders, in narrow trousers that went out of fashion five years back, sporting an unshaved underchin, looking more unkempt than dashing.

He lifted an eyebrow ever so slightly and moved infinitesimally to the left, as though making way for appearance's sake. I waved Amma into the lift as she stepped in awkwardly, unsure of herself, and followed, trying to look confident and extroverted. The liftman didn't move; he waited for further passengers—there was no one in sight—while we fidgeted uneasily, then turned his face a fraction towards me. 'Where to?' he asked.

'The new boutique opening,' Amma answered for me, trying to assert herself. 'In the…er…' she looked at the card—'Plaza Lounge. Which floor is that?'

The liftman looked at her incredulously, then contemptuously. He nodded in sage understanding and made to shut the lift door. In the distant entrance to the hotel foyer, a fat lady in a dress of some expensive material waddled through and the liftman paused in his act for her to make her way to the lift. He could have left us at the first floor and come back for her in that time; but he waited, and so did we. I suddenly felt like rushing out of the lift, the hotel, the area. This wasn't our place. We didn't belong here.

But I didn't. Poor Amma had been so desperately keen on coming to attend the new boutique opening and, despite my reluctance, I had agreed to escort her. Father had a minor desk job in the editorial department of the city's leading paper, and he often got these invitations. He always brought them home proudly as if to show Amma and me he wasn't as much of a failure as we knew he was, and they lay on the solitary bedroom table as cardboard symbols of his prestige. We rarely used them.

But this one time Amma was insistent. She had always been anxious to see how the mod sophisticates she had heard about lived; now here was an opportunity to see them in their natural habitat. She couldn't throw away this chance of a lifetime, and she couldn't go alone. So, she dragged me along.

The fat lady reached the lift and the lift attendant stepped aside in deference to let her in. She was about Amma's age, I guessed; she wore a wig, an excess of make-up, a lot of real-looking jewellery, and an air of haughty superiority. A reek of some expensive perfume preceded her by a good ten yards. Amma stepped back uncomfortably into the darkest recesses of the elevator as she entered.

The lift door shut and the lift proceeded smoothly upwards. I saw Amma trying not to look at the fat lady and I felt a wave of pity and compassion surge up in me. Instinctively, I put a hand on her arm. Don't worry Amma, I thought, I'll protect you. 'Protect you?' the words mocked me in my mind. 'From what?' I hastily dropped my hand from her arm.

The lift stopped, the door opened, and the fat lady stepped out first. It was natural;

unquestioned; it was her due. I let Amma follow and then stepped out too, with a 'thank you' to the liftman. He ignored me completely

Amma was overawed by the landing leading to the suite where the boutique was; the wall-to-wall carpeting, the air-conditioned atmosphere, the little groups of suited-and-booted people. Suddenly even I felt out of my class. I started wishing I had paid more attention to my appearance. I looked into one of the mirrored columns and hastily, furtively, smoothed back my hair.

People were walking into the boutique now. There were not very many of them; perhaps fifteen, perhaps twenty. We were late; the speeches and ribbon-cutting, if there had been any, appeared to be over. People were standing around in twos and threes, sipping coffee served by a uniformed waiter and examining some of the objects for sale. Amma and I hesitantly went in. No one took any notice of us whatsoever.

The waiter passed us, looking through us without pausing in his stride. I thought at first that the coffee had to be paid for, then saw him offering steaming hot cups of it to all the visitors. Anyone who chose to could take a cup of coffee. I felt a wave of anger rising up in me. We had been insulted.

I halted him as he turned back with a half-empty tray by physically standing in his path. 'Here too,' I said. He glowered at me resentfully for a second, then proffered the tray to me. I took a cup and waved him on to Amma. Reluctantly he complied. Amma refused him with a thank you and a smile.

'Why did you do that, Amma?' I asked after the waiter had moved away. 'I thought you liked coffee.' She didn't reply; instead she looked around her and said, 'Come, let's see what there is here.' I followed her to the tastefully decorated section for men's garments.

There were a few people looking at the

clothes put up for sale. A young couple hovered around indecisively and a smiling salesgirl came up to them and asked, 'Can I help you?' They said 'No, thanks,' and she went away. She saw us, equally uncertain, but ignored us all the same.

Amma looked at the impressive array of shirts, ties, and jackets before her. One jacket, in black leather, especially attracted her. 'I've always wanted you to have something like this, son,' she said, 'and God knows we haven't been able to afford to buy you anything. But looking at you in your plain clothes, and seeing these boys here in such fine attire—I want you to have this, I know it will suit you, my son. You are a handsome boy and this will look good on you.' She fingered the sleeve. There was no price tag attached. Poor Amma was captivated by it. I wanted to say no, Amma, I don't want it; I don't need it at all, I am quite content with the clothes I have, but I could imagine myself in that leather jacket, the envy of the boys and the wonder of the girls in the neighbourhood, and no words came out of my lips. I watched her, half in hope and half in anticipation.

Amma caressed the jacket, and took it off its hanger. 'Come closer, my son,' she said, placing it against my body so she could see me with it. 'It looks wonderful. I wonder how much it will cost.'

'Here, you can't touch the articles,' the salesgirl said, coming up behind Amma suddenly. 'Can't you see the sign?' she pointed to a PLEASE DON'T TOUCH card among the clothes. 'Don't you know English?'

Amma flushed a deep red. 'I'm sorry,' she mumbled in confusion, hastily trying to put it back. 'I was just…I didn't see…how much does it cost?'

The salesgirl took the jacket from her hands and looked at her pityingly. 'Seven hundred rupees,' she said.

Amma was completely thrown off her guard by the entirely unexpected figure. 'What... pardon me...seven hundred rupees?' She asked in confused embarrassment.

'That's right, ma'am,' the girl said, placing the jacket back in its place. 'And please don't touch the clothes.'

'It's all right, Amma,' I said. 'I didn't want it anyway. What shall I do with a jacket like this?' Amma still looked miserable, so I added, 'Anyway it's far too big for me—I'd look like a scarecrow in a wrestler's leftovers if I wore this.' She wasn't consoled.

Just then a famous radio disc jockey entered the boutique and all eyes turned in his direction. Tall and ruggedly handsome, he wore a silk shirt and scarf and flared trousers, and I envied him like hell. He strode to the men's suitings salesgirl and said 'Hi.'

'Oh, hello, Jay,' the girl said, 'we've got something you'll really like—the newest thing in ties, and *so* inexpensive. Isn't this one fabulous? And it's *just* seventy.'

'Hmm,' the DJ said in casual approbation, flipping through the ties on the rack. Somehow, I couldn't take my eyes off him. He was everything I wanted to be: impressive, polished, well-dressed, popular—and rich. Amma was looking at him too, sorting the ties out, liking one colour here, objecting to another's width there, and all the while her eyes were travelling from his hands to the PLEASE DON'T TOUCH card nestling unnoticed among the little heap of sartorial rejects at the bottom of the rack. Suddenly I felt physically sick; I wanted to get out of there, get out of the rarefied, air-conditioned atmosphere, out of the wall-to-wall carpeted floor, away from the mirrors on every column that thrust reminders at me of what I really was. A kind of nausea overtook me and momentarily my head swam, converting the floor, the walls, the mirrors, the designs and patterns and decorations and clothes into a whirling, twisting question mark, asking me 'What are you doing here?' And suddenly I realized I didn't know, I didn't know what I was doing there, and the question mark straightened itself out in my mind to an arrow, a line, and I knew where the line led—outside, to the relief of the hot pavements and the elegiac gloom of the evening shut out by the brocaded, mirrored walls of the Plaza Lounge.

'Amma,' I said, clutching her sleeve. 'Let's go.'

But she didn't seem to be listening. There was a strange, semi-determined, half-surprised look on her face and she was moving away from me. I recognized that look; I had often seen it when I had done something wrong at home and she had turned on me, breathing 'ingrate'. Suddenly I realized what she was going to do. I tried to stop her but she had already reached the counter.

'Here,' she was saying in a loud, shrill voice

of complaint, 'I thought we weren't supposed to touch the clothes.'

An offended silence descended upon the congregation. Faces turned to look at us. Amma looked up, a trifle defiantly, expecting an apology or a reprimand but prepared for either, at the salesgirl. The DJ, too, turned from his flirtation with the ties and the women and gave us the benefit of a mildly offended look. Then he turned back and resumed his conversation with the salesgirl. The hubbub of voices around us resumed. The pause was over; our clumsy intrusion had largely been forgotten. But in the harder lines of the salesgirl's face, I knew it would never be forgiven.

'Amma—let's go.' She stood still for a moment, incredulity and hurt writ all over her face, and then slowly, resignedly, without a trace of bitterness or resentment, subsided and walked away from the counter. When she spoke, there was a break in her voice.

'Yes, son—let's…go.'

Quietly, sadly, we walked to the door. No one noticed our exit; it was as if an insect had been removed from a cup of tea, something which ought not to have been there in the first place had been ejected. I evaded the eyes of a passing bearer.

We used the stairs. When we walked out of the hotel and on to the street the ambience was oppressive. I wanted to pick up a brick, a stone, a tile from the pavement, anything, and throw it at the glass front of the building. But I didn't. I couldn't, I didn't have the right to.

'Let's take a taxi, son,' Amma said.

'No, Amma,' I replied and suddenly the lump in my throat wasn't that big any more. 'We'll walk to the bus stop. As usual.'

Something in my tone made her turn and look up at me. I smiled. 'We're going home, Amma,' I said.

I felt the pressure of her hand on my arm as we walked slowly on to join the queue waiting for the bus.

BEST FRIENDS FOREVER
PARO ANAND

'How's my peanut?'

'Did my puchka have a good day?'

'I never expect anything else but the best from you, strawberry.'

Dad always called me by food items. Especially when he was really happy with me. Which, I have to say, was most of the time. Mum, on the other hand, was the more practical one. And yes, you can hear the sneer when I say 'practical'. I mean, I love her and all, she's my mum, after all. But she always called me Saudamini. In this very formal way, almost. No pet names and cute goofy loving terms. This, even when I told her I hated my name. I mean, who, in this day and age, thinks of naming their child after a grandmother? Realllly? There were so many better names out there. Saudamini may have been a great name back then, but now…? Luckily, though, she was one of the few people who called me by my full name. Dad, as I've said, called me by food items.

Dad was really cool, most of the time. He was one of the happiest people I knew. Like, if Mum was annoyed with him, and even if she was being unreasonable (much of the time, I have to say), he'd just apologize and put his arms around her and hold her till the anger went out. Sort of how you throw a blanket over a fire and smother it to cool it. He did it with me too. If Mum and I were in a flaming row, he'd put his arms around us, one at a time, or he'd try and get us both into his wingspan at once, but it didn't work. Not every time at any rate.

Between Mum and me, without his realizing

it, there'd be a simmering resentment left over and that could explode any moment. Mostly, we tried to have our fights when he was away. So that we could fight it out properly and not be smothered into what he hoped was loving silence. But that didn't happen so often. They both worked together in a company that they'd started when they were still at college. So they went off to work together and came back together. And since they'd grown up together, they had all the same friends, so it wasn't as though they'd have a night out with their individual friends.

Although they were childhood friends, they still had their disagreements and as time went by and I hit the teen years, those disagreements turned their gaze more and more on me.

Dad was more the YES parent. He more or else less always said 'yes' when I asked him anything. Whether it was a school trip, a pair of high heels, a sleepover with friends, whatever.

He'd say yes. And that, of course, left Mum to be the NO parent. She'd say no and I'd be left in the middle, hoping Dad would dig his heels in and make her agree with him—with us. But that didn't happen too often. Sometimes, I'd have to prime him for the task. I'd tell him in advance what I was going to ask and I'd make him promise that he was going to stand up for me and not back down to her unreasonableness. But more often than not, when the moment came and she brought her gritted teeth and flashing eyes out, he'd have her in a hug and shrug his shoulders helplessly at me. Sometimes I wished he was more of a man.

I mean, true, why should men be mean, why should they have the ultimate veto? But that's the way most of my friends' homes were. The Dad wore the pants and wielded the veto vote. That's just how it was. But somehow, I ended up with a Dad who was softer and a Mum who was tougher, the one who wore the pants in our home. Not that Dad wore the skirts or saris. Pff, that would be weird.

Sometimes I actually felt a bit sorry for Mum. Not often, but sometimes, she'd look to Dad to be the No and he'd see the look, but turn a blind eye. He was good at that. So I felt for her sometimes. Though, as I've said, not often.

So anyway, it was Mum who first started kicking up a fuss about Aarav coming over. Well, not about his coming over, really, but more that she didn't want us together in my room with the door shut. 'Come over in a group, or sit in the living room,' she'd insist. And my, 'that's so lame', went down as well as one could expect it to. About as well, as the, 'well, I insist', from her did.

Aarav was okay with it, though he did try once with a 'we're just friends' line. But she was having none of it, so he and I sat feeling foolish in our very formal living room, sipping iced tea (of all things, as though we were a hundred and one). We talked awkwardly for about twenty minutes, with Mum pretending she had something very important to do which brought her out through the living room every two minutes (literally, she came in ten times in those twenty minutes). Finally, Aarav said, 'Um, I guess I should go now,' and I said, 'Okay,' almost before the words had left his mouth.

On Mum's eleventh trip through, she feigned surprise and disappointment with a very lame, 'Ohhhh, has he gone already?'

We were bitterly bickering about it when Dad walked in. He'd taken our dog out for a run for about an hour or more.

'Heyyyyy,' he said as soon as he saw us. He didn't need to even hear our fight. Our body language was so battleground. 'What are my two favourite girls talking about? Come here, peanut.' He was already approaching us with his arms stretched out, but he was too sweaty for the hug thing. And frankly, I was just too mad.

Mum turned on him and practically snarled, 'She thinks she's so grown up that she can take boys up to her bedroom and do who knows what behind locked doors....'

'MUM!' I shouted as loudly and fiercely as I could, 'First of all, it's not boys—it's one—my best friend. And secondly, I don't know what you were up to at my age, but all the whatnot I wanted to get up to was talk to my best friend. TALK—just TALK!' I added a 'you sicko' under my breath.

'Then why did you need to lock the door?'

'It wasn't locked, how many times do I have to tell you?'

She gave me her long-suffering sigh and said, 'Fine, then why did you need to *shut* the door?' She turned triumphantly to poor, sweaty Dad so I turned to him too, appealing.

'Because you are in and out of the room like a hundred and twenty times. Like even when we were in the stupid living room, you were hovering like a…like a…' (oh I wanted to say witch or something worse, but I didn't).

'Dad, it's impossible for me to have a proper conversation with anyone if she's around. She won't let me have any privacy. It was soooooo embarrassing.'

There was a moment of silence. We were waiting for Dad's verdict. He slid me a look that I understood immediately. He was telling me that he actually agreed with me but was going to take Mum's side a little, just to soften her up. And also, if he didn't, she'd bite his head right off. Just like a black widow spider.

'So we have no problem with his coming over. It's just that we need you to be careful….' Dad's voice trailed off weakly. Any fool could tell that he wasn't really convinced with his own argument. And Mum was one such. Fool, I mean. She shot him a dirty look, took a deep breath which meant that she was thinking 'Oh lord, I've got to handle this on my own, he's so useless when it comes to being sensible and strict.'

And there, of course, came the lecture for the nth time about how I was not a child any more and there were certain boundaries that had to be maintained between boys and girls now and that raging hormones in teens...blah blah blah!

'Look, I don't know if you've ever even *heard* of a platonic relationship with someone from the opposite *sex*....' Yep, I did emphasize the word as much as I could and got a most satisfactory wince from Mum in return. So I continued, 'But privacy to do *what*?'

I turned to Dad then and appealed to him. But he was already headed towards her with his arms outstretched so she got distracted and shouted at him to stay away. He was sweaty and full of dog hair. They laughed as he chased her. And I really felt that if anyone needed chaperoning it would be them.

I left, really annoyed. This would be a good time to call Aarav. I could chat away, without her hovering.

'I'm really sorry, dude, my mum's just the worst.'

'It's cool, I guess they just don't get that we are really just good friends and it's irrelevant that you're a girl and I, well, I…well, I'm…me.'

And that was enough talk on Mum. We went on to talk about all the other stuff that we'd been wanting to talk about when she was in and out of the room. Nothing earth-shattering, just stuff. That was the best thing about Aarav, we could talk about all kinds of things. Like, he'd even help me decide what to wear to a party. And I never, ever went clothes shopping without him. He had the best taste in clothes. That's the kind of best friend he was.

Anyway, when I came back down, Dad had

worked something like a miracle. He'd hugged a compromise out of Mum that Aarav and I could be in my room, only, we shouldn't shut the door. I had to hug him then, sweat and all. I don't care about not shutting the door. I mean, Aarav and I literally just talk. Unless I'm trying out some new outfit for a party and trying to decide which one I look least hideous in. And even then, I come out of the bathroom and show him. I'm not changing in front of him or anything. I mean, yu-ck.

Anyway, it's nice to be able to chat to him on our own instead of in-the-stupid-living-room thing. Now there is a hot new topic to talk about. I discuss all my crushes with Aarav. And his advice is always great. He doesn't talk much about his love interests. There haven't been many. Or any. Actually. Anyway....

This new boy had just arrived in our class. He was really cute. He's from some other country, some exotic mixed parentage and all of us were dying and vying to get to know more and be his friends. Of course, there were others who got there first, so Aarav and I just had the fleeting pleasure of a nod and a hi, how are you kind of moment.

Later, in my room (finalllly), I confessed to Aarav that I'd fallen in love—also finallllly. This new kid—Daniel—made my heart beat faster, which, in turn, unfortunately made my palms a bit sweaty. 'I think I'm in love, bro. It's not the usual crush this time. I'm sure.'

There was a pause. And it went on a bit and for a terrible long moment, I suddenly had a panic attack wondering if Aarav was in love with me. I mean, he looked so sad. He looked as though the weight of it had suddenly fallen on his shoulders.

'What?' I said, unable to bear the silent tension any more.

'*Nothing….*'

His voice was small and he'd somehow

shrunk. Oh God, he was going to say it. And I loved him. A lot. But I didn't *love* him, love him, you know? What was I going to do? I certainly didn't want to lose my best friend.

'You know you can tell me, Aarav, what is it?' I tried to sound reassuring although I was the one who needed the reassurance myself.

'There, well, there's something I've been needing to talk to you about.'

'Ok…ayyy,' I braced myself. Here it comes. Though inside my head I was saying, 'Shut up, shut up, don't say it. Don't say anything.'

'I…oh man, there's no easy way to say this. Wait, I…oh ma…an.'

He got up, he paced the floor. He turned to me, opened his mouth like, here it comes. But instead, he dropped his shoulders, shook his head, but he wouldn't look at me.

'No, you know, it's nothing, I can't.' But he was near tears now. And honestly, I was kind of relieved that he was backing off. I really didn't want to hear it. Like, if he told me he was in love with me, then…well then, it was going to ruin every single thing in the world. I mean, he couldn't be my best friend any longer. Not once he'd told me he loved me and I didn't love him back.

'Okay, look, don't worry about it. You don't have to tell me if you don't want to.'

He looked at me and I saw the tears leaking out of his eyes. His nose was starting to run, as though the tears were trying to find an alternate route. 'But I need to tell you, I can't lie any more…' his voice was tiny, like a whisper. But a very broken one.

I had to be sensible about this. Even though I'm usually not good at doing practical. That's what was needed now. Bring on the sensible. Bring on the practical.

I didn't know what exactly I was going to say once he told me, but I could not be a friend and then not let him tell me what was weighing him down so much. What kind of friend would that be? He was always such a good listener to my woes. I guess it was my turn now.

'Look, come on, come, sit with me,' I patted the bed for him to come sit. Yeah, he nodded slowly, mouthing the word. He sat on my bed and I got up to shut the door, knowing that Mum was going to come home in a bit and then throw a hissy fit about broken promises, but this was a closed-door talk. I knew that much.

His head was slung so low that his chin was totally resting on his chest. His shoulders were slumped. He looked so small and sad that I knew I was going to really have to help him say it. I stroked his back. His shoulders were so tense.

I leaned my head on his shoulder, kissing the corner of it before laying my head there. He would be more comfortable if I was not looking at him.

'Say it, apple pie,' (getting to be more like my dad every day) I whispered.

'I'm a girl...' he whispered back.

'What?!' I laughed, shoving him with my head. And he actually fell off the bed. I was giggling. 'What d'you mean you're such a girl? You mean that you don't have courage? You mean boys have more courage than girls?' And I was about to launch into this whole woman power spiel, but he held his finger up to shut me up, still looking down at his bare toes.

'No, I didn't say I'm "such a girl", I said, "I am a girl".'

He looked up at me straight in the eye and repeated it.

'I am a girl.'

No, you're not bubbled up inside my throat. I was standing now, though I didn't remember doing that. I thought I had my head on his shoulder. He was still sitting on the floor where he'd fallen when I shoved him.

'Ummm, dude, you don't know what you're talking about. Did you hit your head on something on your way here?'

'Sit down.' Command. He was commanding me to sit on my own bed. I sat. He'd never commanded me before.

'Look, I've been wanting—needing you to know this in a while. I…I…may be a boy by birth. But inside, like who I really am is not a boy, but a girl.'

'No,' was all that came out. I mean, I knew him so well, knew everything about him. How was it remotely possible that I wouldn't know this? Besides, and most important, it just wasn't true. I knew it. Somehow, though, he didn't. So 'NO' was all I could say to him.

Later, much much later, I'm sitting in the living room. My head is on my dad's lap, Mum is stroking my shoulders. And I'm crying my heart out. I haven't even been able to tell them what it's about. But my heart's breaking. It's horrible. Just horrible.

'Something to do with Aarav?' Dad asks.

I nod yes.

'I knew it,' Mum is up and pacing immediately. 'I *just* knew it!' without even looking up, I can feel her turn ferociously onto Dad. Like all of this is his fault.

'I knew it was getting too much. All this best friend stuff is just…just…rubbish.'

'It's not like that, Mum,' I try and butt in. But she's not listening to me any more. I can tell that her imagination has run wild and she's got a horror movie running through her head. And I realize right then that I can't tell them. I don't know how to tell them. And I don't know if they'll understand. Because I don't know how to process what I've just been told. I don't know if I can find the words. Ever.

I feel like I'm on my own. And I've just made it worse for myself by telling them this half truth that something was up between Aarav and me. I cannot, just cannot tell them that my best friend thinks he's a girl. I can't bear to think it myself. But what should I tell them instead? I can't have them thinking that he came on to me. He didn't. He would never. Now I almost wish he had.

And then it strikes me like a ton of bricks. I always thought, somewhere at the back of my stupid brain that Aarav was secretly in love with me. I always somewhere waited for that conversation to come up. And maybe, mayyyyybe, even thought that we could end up together. Like, together, together. And now, well now that…well, that is totally off the table, I find that I am what? A little disappointed? Noooo! Really? Disappointed? Yeah, I have to admit that I kind of am. Hmm…never saw that coming. Or did I?

Okay, now the lie that has to be invented. Why am I so upset with Aarav? What could he have done to make me upset with him but not so much that my parents would stop letting him come over.

Good thing is that I have always been quite a good inventor. Sometimes, I come up with stuff that is even more believable than the truth. Like this one right now.

'Ma, it's not like that, Aarav's my best friend and that's it.'

'Okay, then what is it?'

'Um...actually, there's this new boy in school, he's just come to our class. And I really like him.'

Mum stops her pacing, I can see that she's having a hard time processing that her little daughter is old enough to 'really like guys.' Really, Mom?

'Anyway, when I told Aarav this, he like really disapproved. He didn't want me to pursue this any longer. As though he is, I don't know, my keeper or something. I mean, who is he to say that I can talk to some guy or not?'

The speed of the lie amazes me. I'd be proud if I wasn't so ashamed.

My mum sits down. She has this really pleased expression on her face. I can see that all her reservations about Aarav have flown out the window. She's not the only one out to control her boy-crazy daughter.

'I am sure he has some good reason to ask you to be careful,' Mum says triumphantly.

'Trust your best friend, apple pie,' says Dad, letting out a ball of stress that has obviously been choking him. 'At least you should allow him to express his reservations to you.'

'Yeah...I guess.' I can see they're super surprised that I've given in so easily. But I am not up for more conversation right now. I have a lot of stuff to process. So much in fact that my head is hurting and I think my heart is hurting even more. I can feel it hurting. I can feel my eyes blurring. I've got to get out of the room.

Next thing I know, I'm standing in front of my mirror. I've bunched my hair up into a baseball cap. I'm in my jeans and I've got a hoodie on. I'm trying to look like a boy. Would I ever do that? Would I ever even want to? Remotely? No, I cannot begin to imagine what that would be like. I am a girl. I was born a girl. And I will always be a girl. Of course, sometimes, when it comes to be allowed to stay out after dark, or come home in a cab alone, I have wished I was a boy instead. But that was more a convenience thing. Boys just seem to have it easier, is all.

And I would never actually want it. And I certainly would not in a thousand years do anything about it. It's like, when someone is being really, really irritating, you say, 'I want to kill you,' but you don't actually arm yourself and do anything about it, do you?

Then how come it's different with Aarav? I asked him if it was that he was gay. That's why he liked the new guy. Which, by the way, he had confessed to. He liked the new guy who I liked. IN the SAME way!

But that wasn't it. He seemed so sure. But how can one be sure of such a bizarre thing? It's just not natural. I mean, look, if he was just gay, I would be super cool with it. Okay, maybe not super cool at the beginning, but cool for now and super as soon as I had wrapped my head around it. But this, this was just crazy. Super crazy. Now and forever.

I have seen hijras on the streets. The ones who come begging, banging on your car window. Aggressive. Not like other beggars who will beg and plead. They're so scary. The hijras, I mean. And I've heard that they brutally cut off bits of themselves. The boy bits. How can they do that? Is...is Aarav thinking of something like that? The thought creeps me out so bad. I throw off the cap and yank off the hoodie. I want to be no one but myself. And right now, I want to just puke. And so I do. Puke. My stomach churns with dreadful thoughts. I almost puke my heart out. And afterwards, I feel no better.

How am I going to face him again? How will I look him in the eye? I know one thing. I'm going to have to be cool. No matter what I'm feeling inside, I'm going to have to hold it in. Because I do know that if all this is hard for me, then it's much, much harder for him. He's the one who is going to have to face the world with this. Does he even have a choice? I feel, right now, the best advice I can give him, if any, is to just lump it and not tell anyone else about this.

Maybe there are a lot of other people who have been born wrong. All kinds of wrong. But they just learn to live with it, right? If a person is blind, then they learn how to cope with that—they learn Braille, they get a white cane and whatever. But, basically, in most cases, they have to accept that their blindness is a permanent thing. I think that's what I'm going to tell him to do. Just accept that you're different. That's all. And that you're stuck with being different. That there is nothing you can really do about it.

I feel better now that I know what I'm going to say, how I'm going to face him.

But I felt worse once I said that to him. His face fell. It drained of colour and collapsed. It was as if someone had suddenly shrunk him. Like I'd shrunk him with my words that basically said, 'Just lump it, live with it.'

He turned on his heels and walked away. Without a word. Like I'd let him down and not understood a word. Which was true. I hadn't. I couldn't. How could I? Normal people aren't like this. I mean, have you ever met a hijra in real life? Been friends with one? Yeah, they are out there on the streets harassing people or storming into people's weddings and stuff and making a general nuisance of themselves. Would you ever invite one into your home? Voluntarily? Into your bedroom? Of course not. I am a pretty inclusive person, I am good to all kinds of people and mean to no one. But you have to draw the line somewhere. And hijras are my line.

I knew he'd hate that—being called a hijra. Being called a category of persons. He'd always hated that. That was one of the things I loved about him. I hung my head miserably. Love. The more I came to terms with the fact that I was never going to have a relationship with him beyond being buddies, the more I fell in love with him. This was the most painful thing I had ever been through in my life. In any case,

I didn't even know what that made him. A eunuch, a transgender, a cross-dresser—what??

I googled it. There was so much information. About people who feel it and don't do anything, people who take hormones, people who surgically change themselves.

I had no idea. I felt so stupid, so ignorant.

I wished there was someone I could talk to. But the only one I could talk with was the only one with whom I couldn't. Life was so complicated. And suddenly, all the teen angsty complications seemed so insignificant. What was not being allowed to go for a movie in comparison to this? No comparison.

I called him. I thought maybe I have to do this over the phone. I could not face him right then. He could read my expressions awfully well.

He didn't take my calls. But I persisted. Eventually, he picked up with a gruff hello.

'Hi.'

Pause.

I could hear the eggshells cracking metaphorically as we tried to walk over them.

The prepared speech went flying out of the window.

'What?'

'Just called to say "hey".'

Lame, I know, but it was the best I had.

Long pause got longer. Eggshells cracked some more.

'So you've said "hey". Anything else?'

'Aarav, I'm sorry, I'm really really sorry.'

'You are?'

'I am. I was stupid the way I reacted. I should have, I should have....'

'It's cool, don't worry about it. I don't know what else I expected. It was too weird for you to be okay right away, I should have got that too.'

'Whew....' I felt a gush of relief.

'Whew to you too,' he said, the relief huge for him too.

But then another awkward pause.

A 'where do we go from here?' kind of pause.

'How are you doing?' we said together. And started laughing. It was good to laugh, even though we both knew it was an ineffective band-aid on a ginormous gaping wound. Or something like that.

'I…well…I honestly don't know how I'm doing. I'm freaked out, Aarav. I've never had to deal with anything like this before.'

Honesty is rarely my go-to best policy. But in this one case I knew that was the only card I had left to play.

'I know, I get it. I really do. But you know that I had to tell you. I mean, who else could I go to?'

'Yeah, but Aarav, dude, what are you going to do?'

I wanted to ask him a whole lot of questions about this. Like how long have you known and what in you feels like a girl and are you going to have a surgery or something. My mind was restless with questions, but I didn't know how to ask them. Because honestly, I didn't know if I was ready for the answers.

'Umm, I don't know, I mean, it's the first time I've actually spoken the words out loud....'

'To me?' Whoa, that was a load of responsibility on my shoulders.

'Yep.'

'Your parents?'

'Well, somewhere I think that they may know, or at least suspect something's amiss. But I haven't spoken to them, no.'

'So, you planning to, or just keep it between us?'

'No, I will. I will have to tell them. I can't live like this any longer. I feel, I feel that my life's nothing more than a lie.'

I could feel his heart breaking along with his voice.

'Wanna come over?'

'Listen, I don't think I can do this alone. Will you be with me when I tell them?'

I gulped. I didn't want to be there. I would literally rather be anywhere else on earth when my best friend told his parents that their son wanted to be their daughter instead.

'Sure, of course I'll be with you. Whatever you need.' I said with a mountain more confidence than I felt.

'*Thanks....*'

His voice was small and sad. I could not begin to imagine what he was thinking. I could hardly figure out what I was thinking. What must he be going through? The courage it took for him to tell me. And we'd always shared literally everything.

But I have to do this. I will educate myself and then I will be there. He has to know that I have his back. I do. I will be his forever friend, because he needs me to be.

No, this isn't a blank page left by the printer by mistake. This isn't a mistake. This is what is called a writer's block. Or a lack of solution or resolution.

Because, honestly, this is just me now. Paro Anand. Not Aarav, not Saudamini or any food item.

Why?

Because Paro Anand cannot imagine what it must be like to be in Aarav's shoes. Or Saudamini's shoes. I've tried. I've spent sleepless nights. I know this is something some families face. But I do not know how a friend, especially a child, would react. How does someone like Aarav come to terms with finding out that he is born into the wrong body? How does he come out into the world? This unforgiving world that casts aside people like him?

Oh, I've done my share of research and reading. And soul-searching. But I find that I cannot find myself in those shoes. And fitting into the shoes of the players in my story is an important, essential part of my writing. I can't do it otherwise. The issue of transgender people is a complicated one. There are a lot of technical, biological differences between different kinds of people of this broad group. Too many for me to start describing here. If you are interested, there is information available. This is not the place for me to give it.

Then yesterday, I found myself face to face with a hijra. I was locked in the safety of my air-conditioned car. As I saw the group making their way at the traffic light, I found myself hoping that the light would change before one of them made their way to me. Most of us have felt that way, I think. It's true with most beggars, but with the hijras, there is an added fear.

But it wasn't to be. She knocked on my window. Not too aggressive. And, because I was writing this story, I decided to give her some money. It did not feel right for me to pretend to be asleep behind my sunglasses, which is what I usually do.

I reached into my wallet and pulled out what I thought was a generous hundred. I rolled down my window, making sure to lower it just a little bit (so she couldn't reach in and grab my wallet, as many of us have been told they do). She gave me a big smile. I smiled back and proudly handed the money. But of course, 'these people' are never satisfied with whatever they get, be it a tenner or a hunner. I tried to put my window back up but she knew I'd do that, so she had put her hand in and I almost squeezed her arm off by mistake.

But she was polite. She said she only wanted to bless me. So, I offered the top of my head, feeling admittedly queasy.

She blessed me, she blessed my children as a five hundred note departed from my hand. The lights changed and I somewhere hoped that this little exchange of my trying to be a better human being would unlock the block.

It didn't. It hasn't. There is no way for me to know how to stand in those shoes.

But it's a story that needs to be written. We have been taught to fear hijras, we abhor them, we try and keep them as far as possible from us. And they in turn are aggressive and obnoxious. We wonder why these able-bodied people don't work instead of begging for a living. Never once acknowledging that we don't give a transgender person a job.

Is it our fault? Is it theirs?

I don't know. All I do know is that right now there isn't a solution. To their condition, our conditioning. Or to this story.

But I would love to one day be able to say that I was a better friend to someone like Aarav who found himself quite literally in no-man's land.

Until then. A blank page and a half-written story are the best I have to offer.

THE OWL DELIVERED THE GOOD NEWS ALL NIGHT LONG BUT THE WOODPECKER GOT THE REWARD OF THE GOLDEN CROWN

GAUTAM LAL CHAKMA

Translated from the Chakma by
Lopamudra Maitra Bajpai

This is a story from the old days. There was a severe drought on earth and all plants and animals were on the verge of extinction. The weather had turned harsh and unsuitable for survival and humankind was suffering. The news of this severe condition reached heaven and all the gods were worried. Biyatra, the son of Gangi Ma (Ganga), was worried and descended on earth to witness the condition. He was shocked to see that the trees were standing all bare and dry, the grass had all dried up, and many animals were dead. Only the jagya dumur (Indian fig) tree stood on the banks of the river. Upon seeing this, Biyatra asked the jagya dumur trees if they could provide mankind enough food to keep them alive. The trees replied that they could help sustain mankind. However, this became difficult as all of mankind finished all the fruits of the jagya dumur in two-and-a-half days. This made Biyatra very angry and, in a fit of anger, he kicked the jagya dumur trees. The trees bent down and ever since jagya dumur tend to bend as they grow.

Biyatra kept thinking of how to solve the problem and finally decided that he should persuade Goddess Lakshmi, the deity of prosperity, to come down to earth and bless mankind. He felt that this was the only way to solve the drought problem. He sent Kaliya to heaven to explain to the goddess and ask her to descend on earth. Kaliya went to heaven but got busy drinking alcohol. Soon, he was completely intoxicated and forgot all about his duty until much later when he suddenly remembered his task. He rushed to Goddess Lakshmi, but the goddess, upon seeing the inebriated state of Kaliya, refused to accompany him to earth. Kaliya returned to earth and delivered the news to Biyatra. Biyatra decided to approach Goddess Lakshmi himself and thus, he went to heaven and spoke to the goddess. This time the goddess agreed and soon sent word through the bharati bird about her arrival. The bharati bird was sent down to earth and it informed the owl about Goddess Lakshmi's arrival and also told the owl that all of mankind should be informed of this happy news. The owl, like an obedient messenger, travelled all through the night, hooting and informing everybody about the good news of the goddess's arrival. People heard it all through the night and were very happy. They felt that their anxieties would soon come to an end and they wanted to reward the bird for bringing the happy news. Thus, in the early hours of the morning, all of mankind came out in search of the bird to reward him. However, at that moment, the tired owl had just finished his work and returned to rest within a hollow in the trunk of a tree. None of mankind could spot the owl, but saw another bird instead, a woodpecker hunting for insects and they mistook it for the bird who was the harbinger of good news. They picked up the woodpecker, put him on a special pedestal, and put a golden crown on its head. Then all of mankind worshipped the woodpecker. Thus, to date, the woodpecker has a yellow tuft on its head as a sign of the golden crown that was placed on its head long, long ago.

ACKNOWLEDGEMENTS

Grateful acknowledgement is made to the following copyright holders for permission to reprint copyrighted material in this volume. While every effort has been made to locate and contact copyright holders and obtain permission, this has not always been possible; any inadvertent omissions brought to our notice will be remedied in future editions.

'The Kabuliwallah' by Rabindranath Tagore, translated by Arunava Sinha; translation used with permission of Arunava Sinha.

'Idgah' by Munshi Premchand, translated by Khushwant Singh; translation used with permission of Mala Dayal.

'Portrait of a Lady' by Khushwant Singh used with permission of Mala Dayal.

NOTES ON THE CONTRIBUTORS

Rabindranath Tagore (1861–1941) was the fourteenth son of Debendranath Tagore and Sarada Devi, and started writing early in his life. He joined the Swadeshi Movement against the British in the 1900s. He won the Nobel Prize for Literature in 1913, and used his earnings to partly fund his school and university Visva-Bharati in Santiniketan. His influence on Bengali culture extends far beyond his highly regarded poetry and prose, into music, visual art, and theatre.

Munshi Premchand (1880–1936) was a pioneer of modern Hindi and Urdu fiction. He wrote nearly 300 stories and novels. Among his best-known novels are *Sevasadan*,

Rangmanch, Gaban, Nirmala, and *Godan.* Much of Premchand's best work can be found in his 250 or so short stories, collected in Hindi under the title *Manasarovar.*

Khushwant Singh (1915–2014) was a well-known and widely read author, columnist, and journalist. He was the founder-editor of *Yojana,* and editor of the *Illustrated Weekly of India, National Herald,* and *Hindustan Times.* He wrote several books, including the novels *Train to Pakistan, I Shall Not Hear the Nightingale,* and *Delhi;* his autobiography, *Truth, Love & a Little Malice;* and the two-volume *A History of the Sikhs.* He also translated from Hindi, Urdu, and Punjabi. Khushwant Singh was a member of the Rajya Sabha from 1980 to 1986. In 2007, he was awarded India's second highest civilian honour, the Padma Vibhushan.

Mahasweta Devi (1926–2016), a writer and social activist, was one of India's foremost literary figures in the late twentieth and early twenty-first centuries. During her lifetime, she authored numerous novels, essays, and short stories. In 1996, she received the Jnanpith Award, India's highest literary honour. She was awarded the Ramon Magsaysay Award in 1997 for her 'compassionate crusade through art and activism to claim for tribal peoples a just and honourable place in India's national life'.

Ruskin Bond (b. 1934) is the author of several bestselling novels and collections of short stories, essays, and poems. These include: *The Room on the Roof* (winner of the John Llewellyn Rhys Prize); *Our Trees Still Grow in Dehra* (winner of the Sahitya Akademi Award); and *Miracle at Happy Bazaar* (winner of Kalinga Literary Festival Children's Book of the Year 2021). He was awarded the

Padma Shri in 1999, a Lifetime Achievement Award by the Delhi government in 2012, and the Padma Bhushan in 2014. He has been selected for the prestigious Sahitya Akademi Fellowship 2021.

Stephen Alter (b. 1956) is the author of more than twenty books of fiction and non-fiction. His works of non-fiction include *Wild Himalaya: A Natural History of the Greatest Mountain Range on Earth*, which received the 2020 Banff Mountain Book Award in the Mountain Environment and Natural History category and *Becoming a Mountain: Himalayan Journeys in Search of the Sacred and the Sublime*, which received the Kekoo Naoroji Award for Himalayan Literature. His books of fiction include *In the Jungles of the Night: A Novel about Jim Corbett*, which was shortlisted for the DSC South Asian Literature Award, *Birdwatching: A Novel*, and *The Cloudfarers*, a book for younger readers. He is the founding director of the Mussoorie Mountain Festival.

Shashi Tharoor (b. 1956) is the bestselling author of more than twenty books, both fiction and non-fiction, besides being a noted critic and columnist. His books include *An Era of Darkness: The British Empire in India*, for which he won the Ramnath Goenka Award for Excellence in 2016, for Books (Non-Fiction) and the Sahitya Akademi Award in 2019, and most recently, *Pride, Prejudice and Punditry: The Essential Shashi Tharoor*. He has won numerous literary awards, including a Commonwealth Writers' Prize, and was honoured as New Age Politician of the Year (2010) by NDTV. He was awarded the Pravasi Bharatiya Samman, India's highest honour for overseas Indians. He was given the Crossword Lifetime Achievement Award in 2018.

Paro Anand (b. 1957) writes for children, young adults, and adults. She won the Sahitya Akademi Bal Sahitya Puruskar in 2017 for her anthology *Wild Child* (now published as *Like Smoke*). Her book *No Guns at My Son's Funeral* was on the IBBY Honour List and has been translated into German and Spanish. *The Little Bird Who Held the Sky Up with His Feet* was on 1001 Books to Read Before You Grow Up, an international list of the world's best children's literature. In 2018, she was invited to Harvard Business School's India Conference. She headed the National Centre for Children's Literature, the National Book Trust, India, the apex body for children's literature in India. She also runs a podcast on HubHopper called Literature in Action. She was awarded the Kalinga Karubaki Award for fearless writing in 2019. As a speaker and storyteller, she has represented the country internationally in Sweden, Germany, Singapore, Bhutan,

Bangladesh, the UK, France, and Switzerland, among others.

Gautam Lal Chakma (b. 1960) is editor of *Tripura Sadak*, a Chakma language newspaper published by the Government of Tripura.

Arunava Sinha (b. 1962) translates classic, modern, and contemporary Bengali fiction and non-fiction into English. More than sixty of his translations have been published so far. He has selected and translated *The Greatest Bengali Stories Ever Told* and *The Moving Shadow: Electrifying Bengali Pulp Fiction*. He has won the Crossword Translation Award for Sankar's *Chowringhee* (2007) and Anita Agnihotri's *Seventeen* (2001). He has also won the Muse India Award for his translation of *When the Time is Right* (2012). His translation of *Chowringhee* was shortlisted for The Independent Foreign Fiction Prize (2009). His translations have also been published in the UK, US, Europe, and Asia through further translation.

Lopamudra Maitra Bajpai (b. 1977) is a visual anthropologist, author, and columnist. She works on history, popular culture, and the intangible cultural heritage (ICH) of India and South Asia. She was recently deputed as the Culture Specialist (Research) at the SAARC Cultural Centre, Colombo, Sri Lanka, and has also been a Research Grant Fellow of the Indian High Commission, Sri Lanka. A former Assistant Professor from Symbiosis International Deemed University, Pune, she continues to teach at universities in India and abroad.